AM I TRANS ENOUGH?

of related interest

Yes, You Are Trans Enough
My Transition from Self-Loathing to Self-Love
Mia Violet
ISBN 978 1 78592 315 9
eISBN 978 1 78450 628 5

How to Understand Your Gender
A Practical Guide for Exploring Who You Are
Alex Iantaffi and Meg-John Barker
Foreword by S. Bear Bergman
ISBN 978 1 78592 746 1
eISBN 978 1 78450 517 2

Everything You Ever Wanted to Know about Trans (But Were Afraid to Ask)
Brynn Tannehill
ISBN 978 1 78592 826 0
eISBN 978 1 78450 956 9

Am I Trans Enough?

How to Overcome Your Doubts and Find Your Authentic Self

Alo Johnston

Jessica Kingsley Publishers
London and Philadelphia

First published in Great Britain in 2023 by Jessica Kingsley Publishers
An imprint of Hodder & Stoughton Ltd
An Hachette Company

1

A CIP catalogue record for this title is available from the British Library
and the Library of Congress

ISBN 978 1 83997 534 9
eISBN 978 1 83997 535 6

Printed and bound in Great Britain by Clays Ltd

Jessica Kingsley Publishers' policy is to use papers that are natural,
renewable and recyclable products and made from wood grown in
sustainable forests. The logging and manufacturing processes are expected
to conform to the environmental regulations of the country of origin.

Jessica Kingsley Publishers
Carmelite House
50 Victoria Embankment
London EC4Y 0DZ

www.jkp.com

Contents

Acknowledgments

Thank you to the many people who supported me in the process of writing this book, and helped me develop these ideas:

- To my wife and best friend, Carolyn, who always knew I could write a book, even when I wasn't quite sure it was true.
- To my biological, step, and chosen family for getting me here.
- To my friend and initial editor, Ryan Yates, for helping me create structure out of chaos and encouraging me to keep going.
- To my friends: Eva, Sam, Jensen, Samantha, and Juniper, who all reassured me and supported me along the way.
- To all my trans, nonbinary, and gender nonconforming clients who have shared and trusted me with so much.
- To the people who so graciously allowed me to interview them.
- To the many trans people who came before and taught me so much about gender but, more importantly, helped me realize I could live.

- To my past colleagues at the Los Angeles LGBT Center and the Los Angeles Gender Center.
- To the Los Angeles Department of Recreation and Parks who maintained all the nice picnic tables that were my outdoor writing space early in the pandemic. And to the Los Angeles Public Library that was my indoor writing space later in the pandemic.

Preface

This book grew out of a specific moment in trans history and I hope that by the time you open it you find it outdated. There will come a time when trans identities are accepted to such a degree that trans people are not forced to unlearn the immense amount that we are now required to unlearn in order to accept ourselves. When that day comes, this book will become a historical document, and an amusing if not cringe-worthy one at that. I look forward to that day.

But at the time of writing, we are still in a place of rapid evolution. Discussing trans issues is always complicated due to ever-changing language. Gender-specific language and discourse plants any writing in its specific time and context. The rings of a tree reveal the tree's age and the climate it grew in, and the pages of queer theory reveal the context and politics of the time. What felt groundbreaking in the '70s goes on to feel common knowledge or even outdated in the '90s. Picking up queer theory from the '90s or early 2000s can certainly still be useful, but sometimes it can feel like a snapshot of a different time. Each stage must learn from and build upon its predecessors. Queer and trans people exist within the context of larger society and we are influenced by larger societal changes, and our progress influences the progress of society, and society gives context and shape to our experiences. That is the natural progression. I am telling just one small part of the larger story from where I stand. I am grateful to the trans writers, theorists, clinicians, and ancestors who came before me and lived authentically, which allowed me to write this book.

As you read it, I ask for your graciousness around the language used here. Given a few years, the language may become clunky and obsolete. Given more than a few years, it certainly will be. Feel free to revise the terms as you like while you engage with the ideas.

For now, I define many terms as I go, including psychology-specific terminology, and I include some theory and history for context. While some readers may be familiar with the language around gender identity, I did not want this to be a book that required any background information, or any specific level of education. Hopefully this can reach as many people as possible who need to hear what it contains.

I am intentional about my language and I say what I mean. I mention when something is specific to binary trans people or to nonbinary trans people and when it is relevant to all trans people (binary and nonbinary together). I simply use "trans" as the umbrella term. Mostly I attempt to be as relevant to as many kinds of trans people as possible, but of course gender is so infinite that no book could ever encompass all of it. I use the terms trans masculine/trans feminine, rather than FTM/MTF (female to male/male to female) or AMAB/AFAB (assigned male at birth/assigned female at birth). The terms I use are still imperfect, but they are less focused on birth sex, and currently they are the most widely accepted by the community. There are times when I speak specifically about trans women and trans men and I use those terms, but trans feminine and trans masculine includes nonbinary and binary trans people who may have similar experiences. I use "queer" as an umbrella term for non-heterosexual identities.

I wrote this book from a Western, and sometimes a USA-specific, perspective because that is where I am from and that is where my trans identity and the trans identities of my clients, friends, acquaintances, and colleagues have arisen. I do not claim this is the correct perspective, and I include many critiques of it throughout this book, but it cannot be ignored that this is the context in which many of these ideas grew and what they are fighting back against.

I cite research where possible, and also acknowledge that there are still enormous gaps in the data, and if we wait around for that all to be conducted and published, it will be too late for many. I think there is an immediate need for this information that means you hopefully can forgive me when I need to speak anecdotally. I have made choices to speak generally to protect client confidentiality and also to allow as many people as possible to access these ideas.

All of these are choices that come with pros and cons, and I know there is no way to make the perfect choice for all people, or across time, so again, feel free to revise them as they work for you. I hope that you can take what you like and leave the rest.

Introduction

I spent years of my life asking myself if I was trans enough to transition and if I was trans enough to count. I learned the word "genderqueer" when I was in college and it unlocked something enormous in me, but I had no idea what to do with that feeling. From 20 to 25 years old I would watch every YouTube video I could find from trans and nonbinary people talking about going on hormones and having surgery. I would lurk in countless message boards and online communities searching for answers. For a while I convinced myself I was just fascinated by these people's stories, but eventually it became too hard to maintain a plausible deniability and I knew I wanted someone to tell me if I should transition or not. I wanted to know if it would work out for me and if I would live. It felt life or death, and I know that was not an exaggeration. It was life or death. Everything hinged on whether I was able to figure this out.

I looked for stories that were as close to my own as possible, searching for more and more similarities until I realized I was searching the internet for a video of myself in the future speaking back to my younger and more confused self. I wanted someone to reach through my computer screen and say, "This is who you are, and this is what you need to do." I never found one. Then, in an attempt to keep a balanced perspective and not get my hopes up, I would look up videos of people who had stopped hormones or detransitioned. It seemed to make sense. Maybe I was just pinning all of my hopes on this one thing and I wasn't actually trans. Maybe I just wanted to be trans because at least then I would have a path forward, even if it felt like a horrifying one.

I would think about starting testosterone and would list the few changes that felt exciting and then I would list the much longer list of changes that felt unpleasant and overwhelming. I knew I wanted a deeper voice and more muscle mass, but I was terrified of growing body hair or losing the hair on my head. Looking at the men in my family did not soothe any of those anxieties, and the fears I had seemed to lurk in my genetic makeup, waiting to be unlocked by testosterone. I knew it was impossible to pick and choose which results I would get from hormones, so I would convince myself that there were far more cons than pros and try to put it aside again. This never actually felt like putting it aside so much as trying to stuff the entire contents of my hopes, dreams, and fears into a tiny, dark closet in the back of my brain and hoping the closet door would not explode open from overcrowding. The stretches of time where I felt okay became shorter and shorter, and the occurrence of what I started to call "gender panic attacks" got closer and closer together. The gender panic attacks were when that closet burst open unexpectedly because I had gently brushed past some miniscule gender trigger. The triggers got smaller and the panic got larger. Eventually I could not stop thinking about hormones. I knew I had reached the limits of where my imagination could take me and I would have to try testosterone in order to find out how I would feel on it. I couldn't imagine what it would do to my body physically and I certainly couldn't imagine how it would make me feel mentally or emotionally.

Making that decision felt like jumping off a cliff. I was afraid of having to live life as a trans person and I was afraid of finding out that transition wouldn't save me. I had been white-knuckling life knowing that it was unsustainable and that something drastic had to change in order for me to make it to old age. I wasn't actively suicidal in the same ways I had heard people discuss suicide, but I had made detailed plans that always started with "If things don't get better by the time I'm thirty, then I can't keep doing this..."

At that time, I lived in Los Angeles and sought out an informed consent clinic' to start the process of getting on hormones. I knew I wouldn't be able to convince a doctor or therapist that I was trans because I didn't know if I was. I just knew I had to try. I did the blood test, I signed the packet of forms that notified me of what to expect and what sorts of side effects might exist, and eventually I got my prescription. I received my supplies and testosterone in the mail in about a week.

Five minutes after my first testosterone injection was the first time in my entire life I truly thought, *What if this works for me? What if this is actually what I need? What if this does change my life for the better?* Needless to say, nothing physically had happened to me after five minutes on testosterone. My voice hadn't gotten deeper and I was far from seeing increased muscle mass. But I think there was something about the testosterone being in my body (and it being unremovable) that allowed me to stop focusing on all my fears and allowed me to focus on my hopes for the first time. As much as I thought I had been doing that consciously for the past five years, really I had been so terrified of being wrong that I had not truly known what optimism even felt like. I had not been balancing hope and fear, idealism and discretion; I had been feeding my fears and suffocating my hope. I had been so careful to "balance" the positive stories with the negative stories that I hadn't noticed that throughout my whole life I had been fed negative stories about transition and that the whole scale was wildly unbalanced from the start. It turned out that my worst fears about physical changes were because of the limitations of my imagination. I could not imagine the fullness of my experience as an embodied and happy adult. The only way for me to know what that felt like was to experience it for myself.

I imagine you have come to this book with many of your own questions of if you are trans enough and what you are supposed to do with your endless thoughts about gender. I imagine many of you are somewhere in the online lurking phase of questioning, or at the stage where you are still half convinced that you are just incredibly fascinated with the concept of gender on a theoretical level. Perhaps you have been living with an increasing sense of unease in your life and have never been able to figure out what it is and have some inkling it might be about your body or your identity. Maybe you have already decided, *Yeah maybe I'm nonbinary/transgender but I'm fine, I think I can just ignore that forever*, and then you have your twelfth panic attack this month about the neckline of your shirt. Maybe taking any steps toward social or medical transition seems too overwhelming and would break your parents' hearts, so you have just decided to take this with you to your grave. Maybe sometimes you think, *Sure, I want some of those transition effects, but I'm not like those real trans people with real dysphoria, so I'm probably just appropriating the trans experience.* Maybe you think your experience might actually just be internalized misogyny or a fetish. If any of those things sound familiar, then you have come to the right place.

As much as you might like to look to an external source for verification and validation, there is no such thing. There is no saliva, urine, or blood test to tell you if you are positive for The Trans. There is no MRI, EEG, or PET scan to detect it. It's actually a very good thing there aren't those tests, but sometimes it can feel like a horrible and confusing burden. It can feel impossible to assess your own internal experience of gender when it is all subjective and therefore susceptible to all of your self-doubt and second-guessing. How can you be sure? How can you validate yourself?

I can give you one small piece of information right now. If you have ever asked yourself, "Am I trans enough?," the answer is undoubtedly yes. You are. I hope this is great news and a relief, but if it does not feel like great news, that is okay too. If your immediate response to that statement is resistance, that is also fine. It is okay if you do not feel trans enough yet or have no idea if you are trans at all. Stick with this for a while and see what comes up for you.

Perhaps try reading this book while gently holding the question "What if this was relevant to my experience?" and simply staying open to what might come from it. You don't have to act on any of this; you are not required to take any steps or actions regardless of what you decide at the end. But know that even if you only decide you are trans in your own mind and never speak it out loud to anyone, your experience is just as welcome and valid as anyone else's. For better or worse, there is no ignoring your thoughts. If you try to ignore them, they will pop up at the most inconvenient moments and only get louder and louder. Which means whether this results in outward action or not, the only way out is through. The only way to not stay trapped in the loop your brain is circling day in and day out is to stop and look directly at it. And it also may mean that things will get worse before they get better. But you are far stronger than you think, and I hope you have the continued courage to keep reading and find out what is within you.

This book is not a workbook[2] or a guide, and once you finish it, you will not have a five-year plan. This book is about all the barriers that are most likely in the way of you reaching your most authentic self without you even knowing it and how to begin to address them. It is split into four parts that address what is likely impeding your internal progress (Part I), some of the historical narratives that are contributing to those thoughts (Part II), how to address some of the mental health effects that may have stemmed from them (Part III), and how they might be affecting your interpersonal relationships (Part IV). This book might be better described as a philosophical self-help book.

As a therapist and a trans person, I believe there is a great amount of power in being able to reclaim our own experiences back from a cisgender perspective, so this book is from a trans perspective for the trans and questioning communities. It is born out of thousands of hours of discussions with hundreds of trans people. It is a collection of what works and a rejection of what feels like it should work but does not.

As I have worked with my trans and questioning clients, I have found that there are reappearing barriers and mental blocks that consistently keep people stuck in mental loops, and there are very few people discussing these ideas publicly. Many resources seek to educate and soothe the fears of cis people, and there are few that are directed to trans people and their concerns. As much as I think there is a need for resources for allies, I think the kinds of messages that are necessary to reassure cisgender people do a disservice to trans and questioning people. When we focus on an outside cisgender audience, then we can censor the kinds of stories that are the most useful for trans people to hear. Attempting to create that clean narrative around gender and transition for cis people erases the more complicated and nuanced experiences that need to be told. Parts of this book will be controversial and there is a lot of space for debate, but I hope it creates much-needed space for trans people to engage with their fears and doubts without the pressure of appearing to be a perfect trans representative.

Primarily, I wrote this book to serve and benefit the trans community above all else. I have written it to help you see that you are not alone, and you are not the first person to have these questions and these doubts. There are many people who have walked this path before you, and they were just as scared and unsure. While there is no map, I hope I can save you the time of walking in circles.

PART I

The Personal and Philosophy

Let's start this book with what's inside of you. If you picked this up wanting to know the answer to "Am I trans enough?," then I'm sure you're anxious to reach the answer and understand yourself and your needs. But in order to reach it, you first have to know what you're up against.

Why is this such a difficult question to answer? How do you assess your identity and then claim your decision? Are you even allowed to decide that for yourself? These are not insignificant questions, and there is a lot getting in your way that you may not even be aware of.

In Part I, we will break down what you are carrying around and how those thoughts and feelings got there in the first place. The better you know what you're up against, the better you will be able to fight it.

By the end of this section, you will understand the burdens you've been carrying and will have already started the work of unburdening yourself.

CHAPTER 1

What Are Narratives but the Stories We Tell?

We are made up of the stories that we are told and the stories we tell ourselves. We are made up of new stories and ones that have been handed down for generations. Sometimes those stories are close to the truth, and sometimes they are intentionally or unintentionally meant to affect our behavior and actions. And yet when we are born, no one shares all of these stories with us. It can take decades to even discover your family history and what your place is in the story of your parents and grandparents and great-grandparents. What is the emotional story of your family, what is the immigration story, what is the regional story, what is the cultural story, what are the beliefs about money and religion and love and obligation that exist from the people who raised you? This process can be a slow unearthing that may never become fully clear. It can be a privilege to even have the information to create a narrative of your existence and your self.

In some ways, the word "narrative" is just a fancy word for a story. In some ways it implies more about how the story is being told and what choices are being made to include or exclude certain pieces of information.

Think of how many World War II movies and documentaries and books you have seen, or you have read, or you have channel-surfed past, or some guy has tried to make you watch. Someone right this second is probably filming another WWII movie. There are many reasons for this, including privileging certain European and American perspectives, but also because a whole lot happened during that war, and you could never tell it all in any single book or movie. Depending on if you decide to focus on Winston Churchill or Adolf Hitler or a single French soldier or a Soviet sniper, you will have entirely different details and perspectives and beginnings, middles, and ends. What if you told a World War II story from the perspective of someone who did not know World War II was occurring?

If you read a world history book, you are not going to get every detail about everything that has ever happened. Instead, you will get big events and patterns and their supposed meaning. You will also get bias. You may have taken a world history class and found you learned nothing about African history except when it was relevant to white European or North American history. In other words, you will hear African history through the lens of non-African people and people who believed that the history of Africa is not important on its own terms. Many places in the world do not seem to exist in the world history narrative until they are colonized. Their stories do not come into frame until they meet up with the stories of those who are considered the main characters. No surprise, when white Europeans are writing world history, they believe they are the main characters. They also tend to believe they are the good guys. Residents of colonized countries have a very different take on that. But what happens if you never speak to other people or read their stories? When that happens, it is easy to miss important details and alternate views. We lose sight of a complete image and start to believe that the single story we have heard is absolutely true and everyone believes it. This is very dangerous and also subtly insidious.

Who is in charge of telling the story and what do their biases and blind spots mean when they are passed on? What narratives do we have that are just the insecurities and shortcomings of groups of people in charge of writing down history?

The narratives around gender have had many authors, and many of those narratives have been passed down as universal truths. Ideas around what are appropriate ways of living are explained as if they are biological truths, and the further we dig, the more we find that there is a great deal being left out of the narrative. Trans and intersex people can point out massive flaws in the narrative simply by existing and living authentically. That is quite a burden when you are transgender and/or intersex and deconstructing cultural narratives was not something you signed on for. No baby is born with the life mission of taking on challenging the societal narratives of something as large as gender and sex. Trans people are just as likely as anyone else to internalize the narratives around gender, and then they must go through a process of excavating those false and unhelpful narratives.

Internalizing a narrative is the process of taking the external narratives you have been and are being told and placing them inside yourself. This can also lead to restricting and policing yourself. It can be easy to forget that a narrative is simply a story and it is not necessarily objective truth. Only after many years of punishing yourself with them does it sometimes become apparent that there is another way, perhaps even a better way.

For example, take the narrative around gender dysphoria. Much of the medical and psychological criteria around trans identities exists around the idea of gender dysphoria. Dysphoria is defined by the Oxford English Dictionary simply as a "state or condition marked by feelings of unease or (mental) discomfort." It comes from a Greek word meaning "hard to bear." The term dysphoria itself is not commonly used by many people outside of the context of gender, so it can begin to take on the feel of a very specific and clinical term. But the word does exist outside of a clinical context. It is the counterpoint to the word euphoria, which comes from the Greek word meaning "bearing well."

Members of the trans community who have felt unincluded or misrepresented by a definition of trans identities that focuses exclusively on gender dysphoria have popularized the concept of gender euphoria. As you might expect, this is the concept of feeling correct and even pleased in a gender presentation or experience. For example, a trans woman could feel gender euphoria at being referred to as "ma'am" in a grocery store. Some nonbinary people even experience gender euphoria not by being seen "correctly" but by confusing people who are unsure of how to gender them. This is of course not all nonbinary people, but it is simply to say that the experience of gender euphoria does not necessarily hinge on being seen correctly. It is simply that the experience feels right to their internal sense of self.

Gender dysphoria and gender euphoria then can be seen as two sides of the same coin, where dysphoria focuses on the worse and the euphoria focuses on the better. Experiencing gender euphoria means you are experiencing something that feels better than past experiences. You could certainly call those past experiences dysphoria, but it is likely that many people don't because it can be hard to know that something feels wrong until you have the contrary experience of something feeling right. It is not always easy to identify in the moment if something feels wrong or off because it may have always felt wrong or off, and then you have a real "How does a fish know it's wet?" situation.

Some trans people relate more to a narrative of dysphoria and some relate more to a narrative of euphoria, and some relate to both in different contexts. But there are also many people who are not aware that the alternate narrative of gender euphoria exists because the narrative of gender dysphoria has dominated the conversation for so long. It was the terminology used by the supposed experts and therefore was the framing all trans people were required to take on until someone asked why and proposed an alternative. Regardless of if the whole world accepts that new narrative or not, it can certainly have a life-changing effect for the person who questions it for themselves.

CHAPTER 2

Internalizing Transphobia

The existence of transgender people threatens narratives that many people hold near and dear to their hearts. Namely that bodies determine gender, which determine gender roles, which determine destiny. In other words, the body parts you are born with are going to determine the kind of person you are going to become, and the kind of person you become is stagnant. This narrative allows strict gender roles around men and women. It says that women's bodies make them weak and less capable than men. The specifics of this idea change with each era, but the conclusion is always the same: Men have to be in charge for biological reasons. They're natural leaders! They're natural protectors! They're natural warriors! They're the reason the whole world hasn't devolved into chaos! Again, the specifics don't matter as much as the hierarchy that gets created. Cisgender men want to be on top of that hierarchy and they have enforced their place through violence when anyone has challenged it. But bodies determining gender, and therefore gender roles, on their own are not good enough. This narrative also requires that each position is fixed. Men are men and women are women. There's no moving around once you're placed in the hierarchy. Men do manly things and have the power, and women do what men want them to do and don't have any power. Challenging that hierarchy would obviously be an issue for the men who want to keep their position on top. And trans people throw a wrench into just about every part of this machine. Trans people show that body parts do not determine gender or gender roles or destiny. This is extremely inconvenient!

When trans people show up to fuck up your nice little pyramid of power (or your house of cards), you can do a few things to neutralize that threat to the status quo. The first is to erase the existence of transgender people and pretend they do not exist. This can work for a little while, but eventually people catch on that trans people are everywhere. Then when that stops working, you can convince them that there are correct kinds of trans people and incorrect kinds of trans people. You do this by convincing people that cisgender bodies are morally good and correct and transgender people should aspire to have bodies as close as possible to what is morally good and correct. You can convince them that the closer they are to cisgender people, the more acceptable they are and the more power you might send their way if they behave. You can make them fight amongst themselves about who is the right kind of trans person and who is the wrong kind of trans person, and fight over the scraps of resources.

If you're lucky, the trans community will be so busy doing this that they won't notice that you are actually hoarding power for arbitrary reasons. Then the masterful last step is getting trans people to internalize these beliefs and enforce them in themselves and within their own community. Once you've done that, then you barely need to do any work to keep the whole system functioning as intended.

And historically this is exactly what has happened. When Western medicine officially acknowledged transgender people, there were many official and unofficial expectations. Trans people were expected to be:

- binary (male to female or female to male)
- straight
- fulfilling traditional gender roles and presentation
- interested in complete social, legal, and medical transition
- cisgender-passing (or wanting to be cis-passing)
- dysphoric until medical transition is complete.

Until finally they are assimilated into cis culture, where they are asked to disappear and stop challenging the power structures.

I have a feeling you looked at this list and thought, *Damn, I don't know a single trans person who is all of those things.* And I don't either. This is not a real trans person. This is the fantasy of a palatable trans person. It is a model of the inoffensive. Trans people are boundless and not limited to the imaginations of cis people, and yet this cis-centric society hinges on limitations. It requires that we see our trans identities as a burden and a disorder until we can take the necessary steps to appear as cis as possible. Because being cis must be the norm in order for the gender hierarchy to be the norm. The gender hierarchy requires people on top and people on bottom, and there is no space for movement. Because if people are able to move up and down the ladder, then we must acknowledge that placement is not based on inherent and permanent features of bodies.

If you've ever wondered why trans people make cis people so mad, you can now see that it is because it threatens the arbitrariness of what has constrained their lives. No one wants to discover that the hierarchy that says they're lesser doesn't need to exist and is based on nothing. On the other end, no one wants to discover that the reason they are given power is not based on any of their skills or knowledge. Being born with a specific set of genitalia does not determine your role or interests or personality, and it does not determine who you must become or who you must remain. It actually determines almost nothing at all.

But if everyone began to realize that gender does not equal destiny, then the house of cards will fall, and this can't happen. Forcing trans people to internalize these expectations is further violence to maintain the status quo. These expectations constrain trans people who are out, but they also impede people who are questioning their gender. Keeping the number of trans people low keeps the threat to the system low. If you can get people to doubt if they will ever be trans enough, then they will police themselves for you, and that's exactly the point. This is our foundation of doubt, but it is certainly not the extent of it.

CHAPTER 3

The Leap of Faith

Almost everyone approaches the question of "What if I'm trans?" with a feeling of dread and terror. You don't need a lot of context to know that being trans is deeply stigmatized, and living as a trans person is not easy. It is safe to say that most trans people initially question their gender the same way they would enter a haunted house: *There better not be anything that is going to jump out at me from the shadows or I will scream.*

And the risk feels so high. We find ourselves standing smack dab in the middle of a societal narrative that states that transition is one of the most extreme things you could do with your body. As we have already discussed, society asks you not to be trans, but if you must, then you damn well better be sure about it. And medical transition? Then you are going to need to make that 110 percent sure. But how can you possibly feel sure? And how do you prove that you are sure to a doctor or therapist or judge when you are so full of doubt? How can an internal felt sense be quantified and verified by an external party?

There is no easy answer. Historically the answer has been that gatekeepers demand a show of extreme distress (or dysphoria) to prove that you are the right kind of trans person. They have created strict standards in order to determine who *really* is trans versus those others they deem fakers or people plagued by other mental health issues. In the past there have been trials like the "real-life test," where trans people were asked to "publicly live and dress as a man/woman" for one year in order to show that they would not regret a decision to medically transition. Of course, what actually happened was that trans people had to walk down the street and go to work and live their daily lives dressed as their gender without the assistance of the medical transition they were trying to access in the first place. This led to scrutiny and sometimes violence by cisgender people, who were given a whole year to gawk. What an incredible burden! It's no wonder that many people weren't willing to endure that much humiliation. What these kinds of standards really communicated was "No person would ever undergo this test by choice, so if you go through with it, then you must be really serious." It was less of a choice and more of a gamble. Trans people were forced to decide if the possible better future was worth the terrifying and dangerous present.

The real-life test is no longer considered best practice and has mostly been abandoned by clinicians and medical providers, but the message within our society has remained nearly the same: You have to be near death in order for cisgender gatekeepers to approve and facilitate a gender transition. Transitioning is seen as an allowable course of action if you are near death. Even now, shockingly high suicide statistics are still a primary tool to make cis people understand why trans care is necessary in the first place. Instead of "people will feel better," it must be taken to the extreme of "if we do not allow them to do this, they will kill themselves." There is nothing more certain than that.

But obviously this kind of system does not function well

to actually care for all trans people. It only addresses a fraction of the trans people and gender-questioning people who are seeking care. It instead functions to limit "risk" as defined by the gatekeepers, and to limit trans people. It functions to prevent malpractice lawsuits (supposedly). It limits the number of trans people with access to care to an extremely tiny percentage of people who can imitate certainty through extreme distress. (Because spoiler alert: No one is certain.) This means we have a tiny trickle of all the trans people getting through the obstacle course of doctor's appointments, therapist/psychiatrist appointments, and judges and so on. But then what happens to everyone else who does not meet that threshold of certainty?

Either they become so distressed by the process of not getting through that they reach the threshold or they are deemed "not trans enough" by some outside official. That official designation of "not trans enough" is insidious and can do immense harm in the long term. It can mean that someone seeking out access to transition-related care in their teens or 20s ends up being someone who appears to be a case of "failure to launch" and then returns to therapeutic care decades later, still dealing with all the same difficulties and confusion as before but they have become much more severe. These are the pathways for a trans person in a gatekeeper model: prove immense distress and access care; fail to prove immense distress and then become distressed in the short term; or fail to prove immense distress and become distressed in the long term. The final option is the most discouraging of all. It is when someone fails to prove immense distress and a clinician convinces them that what they are experiencing is not gender related at all and is actually some other medical or mental illness. This is one pathway to death.

This means that gatekeepers create a self-fulfilling prophecy.

The less accessible you make transition, the more desperate, dysphoric, and suicidal people become. Gatekeepers create what they expect and want to see, whether they believe they are doing this or not. By expecting to see distress, they create distress.

Imagine an alternate society where everyone was encouraged to explore their gender identity from a young age and people did not make assumptions about your future in the first seconds you are breathing air based on your genitals. There would still be a whole lot of cisgender people (although I would argue there would be a lot healthier and more authentic versions of cisgender people). There would be far more binary trans people as well, because those trans people would have grown up always knowing that it was an option available and accessible to them. Finally there would also be a whole lot of nonbinary people, far more than there are now. Why? Because when you go from two choices to millions, if not billions, of options, you are going to find that a lot of people find their comfort outside of the two initially proposed options. In this alternate society, there would be far less distress because no one is forced into the wrong box and then forced to escape it. No one is forced to argue with their family, teachers, strangers, doctors, or anyone else that their gender is something other than what those people think it is. It would be just a whole lot less work. The part of the trans experience that is distressing is how much fucking work it is to be seen. How endlessly exhausting it is to be consistently fighting for the most basic acknowledgment and respect. Without all of that, extreme dysphoria and distress to the point of suicidal ideation would not be the primary defining characteristic of the trans experience.

Now you ask: *But aren't things better than they used to be?*

And the answer is yes, but how much depends on a lot of factors. There is now another option for accessing care in many places. Depending on where you live, you may have access to informed consent treatment. This now means that people can try hormones and find out if they are right for them. This scares the shit out of lots of cis people. The old narratives sometimes get even louder in light of this expanded access. In their fear and concern, cis people keep shouting about how these changes are permanent and you have to be sure or you could be making a terrible mistake. They shout that you are ruining your body, or there is no way to know so young. Or maybe they shout that you cannot transition so old; if you were really trans, you would have transitioned when you were younger. They latch onto stories about "transtrenders" (or people who are supposedly transitioning because it is the cool thing to do) and people who detransition. They try to find as much evidence as they can about people who have regretted their surgeries. What all of this really comes down to is their concern of not understanding how anyone could want that for themselves, and their fear about what it means about the arbitrary gender roles they were handed. That is fine for them; they do not have to understand (although this is easier said than believed). But no matter what, the more we hear those messages, the more we internalize them.

We start to put that threshold of certainty on ourselves even when there is not an actual outside gatekeeper. We become our own gatekeepers. Trans people become gatekeepers to other trans people. And to get back to our last spoiler: That certainty is an illusion. No one is sure. No one.

Let me say that again: *No one is sure.*

I am sure your mind has already jumped to one (if not a

dozen) trans person you have seen on TV, or on social media, who is definitely, absolutely, completely sure about their transition and always has been. I can assure you that they have not been sure every step of the way, because this is not possible. The human mind cannot look at a change so enormous as to affect your whole-ass life and its countless unknowns and go, *Yeah, we definitely got this, no doubts whatsoever.*

More importantly still, our culture accepts uncertainty and changed minds about big decisions all the time. We know that people change and evolve constantly. People get divorced, people move across the country, people drop out of school, people get plastic surgery to fix their plastic surgery, people change careers. I am not claiming that those people changing the course of their lives don't feel shame and embarrassment sometimes when they realize what they wanted might actually be different than what they thought they wanted, and I'm not claiming that there aren't people in their lives who strongly discourage them from doing so. I am only claiming that most of the time society does not forbid divorce or forever shun someone who has been divorced. Some individuals may, some churches may, and even some cultures may, but society on the whole has made a space for divorce to be discussed and portrayed. It is a common enough experience that you will see it portrayed in movies and shows and books. It is an experience that people are understood to have and can move forward from. Even in some of those same churches that shun divorce it can still be allowed! And sometimes the reaction is as simple as "you tried marriage and you didn't know what it would bring."

Society has not gotten there when it comes to transition and trans identities. It is expected that you are sure, and if it turns out you were "wrong," then this is seen as confirmation that this was a terrible set of decisions you made in the first place. But the reality for many trans people is there no way to know if some of these big changes, like hormone therapy, will make us feel better without trying them. Trying to think about it, and imagine it, and fantasize about it eventually stops being useful because there are too many unknowns. It is an equation of all variables, and you cannot solve an equation of all variables. You have to put actual numbers and data in. How do you get that data? By conducting the experiment. Not by setting up the experiment and then walking away. Not by doing the first two steps of the experiment and then assuming it is a failed attempt. By following through with it long enough to find out: Is this better or is this worse?

Perhaps it feels less like a well set up experiment and more like the game of "hotter or colder" you might have played as a child. Usually someone is blindfolded and trying to find something or someone, and other children direct the seeker by saying "hotter" when they get closer to the goal or "colder" when they get further away. This can result in the seeker wandering around with their arms outstretched trying to not bump into too many things or trip over anything. It is far from the kind of direct instructions that might feel useful, like take three steps to the left and then walk forward ten steps. In fact, if this was actually about efficiency, it would be much more helpful to have a map and not a blindfold. But in this game and in the process of working to understand your gender identity, no one has a map and we all have the blindfold of the cis-centric narratives that we have internalized. The way to find your personalized goal is by stepping into different spaces and determining how you feel in them and if you like them. And while people tend to believe that any time they reach a space that feels wrong and their brain starts shouting "Colder! Colder!" as an embarrassing mistake or a regression, it is actually just a different kind of information. Information about what you do not like and do not want is also critical to have. It does not usually feel as satisfying as the positive information or the epiphany that most people would like to have but it is information nonetheless, and it starts to give you a smaller area to seek out what you do truly want and need.

Crossing the divide from uncertainty (where everyone begins) to information that leads to eventual certainty is a leap of faith. There is no way to think and consider your way across to that certainty. There is no way to make tiny incremental changes that feel safe each and every step of the way. There is only trial and error, and some of it will feel like you are taking a risk because the effect is unknown. And maybe that eventual certainty is not what you thought it was going to be. Maybe you thought you were a binary trans person and it turns out you are nonbinary, or vice versa. Maybe you thought you wanted no medical aspects of transition and it turns out you want some, or vice versa. Sometimes the answers are not what we expect. Regardless, you are worthy of having the answers. You deserve to have them so you can stop wondering and begin to live the life where you know.

CHAPTER 4

Inaction Is Not a Neutral Decision

O ften when an adolescent comes out as trans, parents respond by telling them that they can do whatever they want with their bodies once they become a legal adult. Once someone takes the step from self-identifying with language to what is seen as making irreversible changes, then there is a demand to hold off until adulthood. This concession is not usually based on the fact that the difference between being 17 years and 364 days old is developmentally not any different than being 18 years old (or whatever the age of majority is in your country) but instead is because the parent is admitting that this is not something they approve of but they acknowledge they would no longer have legal control over their child's body at that time. It also is based on the belief that waiting is relatively harmless, or perhaps in the parent's mind, that waiting is less harmful than physically transitioning would be. Of course the parent has other thoughts, feelings, and internal biases as well, but in order to tell someone that they should wait you must believe that waiting is a somewhat neutral decision. In fact, many people believe that waiting is neutral, and that neutrality is possible.

This hinges on the fact that transitioning is seen as action, while waiting is seen as inaction. It is believed that people are just living their lives and the decision to transition or not is one where you either continue along as you were or you suddenly change everything. Particularly for adolescents who are in the midst of puberty, transition is seen as a time where that "normal development" is derailed and something entirely new is put in its place. Even something like puberty blockers can be seen as derailing the process of normal development.

While there is more and more research that shows that puberty blockers are immensely safe on a medical level, and incredibly beneficial to the mental health of trans youth, parents often struggle to feel comfortable allowing their child to start on blockers. As you would assume from the name, puberty blockers essentially just put the changes of puberty on hold. They are not permanent, and eventually the adolescent must either go through a testosterone- or estrogen-dominant puberty (whether that means going through the process of natal puberty or it means hormone therapy), but blockers provide more time to become comfortable or make a decision. I can comfortably say it is usually the parent who needs more time and not the adolescent, but regardless, blockers put things on pause and allow more time for a decision. Blockers are necessary because for a trans adolescent, the changes of their natal puberty are not neutral. For a trans feminine adolescent, a natal puberty brings changes like their voice deepening and skeletal changes like increased height and shoulders widening. For a trans masculine adolescent, the development of breasts or the widening of their hips can be extremely distressing. These changes are either permanent (in the case of skeletal changes like height), or ones that can only be changed through future surgery (such as breast development). This means for a trans adolescent who is aware of their trans identity, being told to potentially wait for years to begin the process of transition also means watching continued physical development in a distressing and dysphoria-inducing direction. Puberty becomes a time when trans adolescents become increasingly anxious, depressed, and even suicidal. In other words, unimpeded puberty is not a neutral decision for the trans person. It is very much the opposite.

This is extremely important for the parents of trans children and adolescents to understand, but even for trans adults who were not aware of their trans identities during the process of their initial puberty it is a narrative that becomes internalized. Trans adults can also believe that continuing on their current path of uninterrupted physical and social development is a neutral decision, while deciding to transition is seen as one that would derail their life and put them on a separate path entirely. It feels as though making a decision to transition is unnaturally halting the momentum of life and starting something else entirely. Sometimes people see this as trans people playing God.

Even if you don't believe in God or the concepts of fate or destiny, it becomes easy to get caught up in the idea that there is one way that your life *should* go and conversely there is an option where you violently wrest control away from The Fates. Of course, there is no way your life should go. There is no script to stick to or stray from and there is no one keeping score of whether you hit all the markers of your life's potential at the intended pace. But we get stuck believing there is a series of options that constitute the kind of life we should have and then there is some other unauthorized or reckless version. Why is it that so many of us believe this?

I suspect it is easier to believe that the suffering from attempting to be cis was meaningful and important than it is to believe that the suffering could just have been painful and unnecessary. If we can believe that being cis was the right way for our life to go, then we can believe that we were striving to achieve something difficult, rather than something arbitrary. We can actually go from allowing inaction to feel like the safest and most neutral decision to determining that it actually was a superior one. It's a useful and protective belief to hold during those many years of unease or pain or distress.

Whether we realize it or not, this can become a martyr complex. That martyr complex tells us that our suffering is admirable or just or holy or a show of quiet strength. It tells us that the long-term suffering has made us morally strong or resilient. And for that reason, being a martyr can feel easier than just being a person who has been hurt. Acknowledging the hurt means feeling the hurt.

But suffering is not admirable on its own terms. And not transitioning is not admirable on its own terms. Because in order for that to be true, then it would require that being cis is in some way morally superior to being trans. I personally don't believe that is true, and I hope now that you consciously don't either. If you're unsure, I would like to ask what it would mean for being cis or trans to be morally superior. What could give some genders that kind of power and not others? What would it mean for a gender to be morally inferior?

Regardless of your answers, hopefully we can both agree on one thing: A truly moral act is to care for yourself. It is a moral act to determine your own needs so that you can fulfill them. It is a moral act to acknowledge that you are just as worthy of having your needs met as any other human being on this earth. You are not so special as to be unworthy.

CHAPTER 5

The Paradox of Transition

When you ask a lot of trans people why they came out or transitioned, you will get a lot of answers about how people wanted to be true to themselves, how they wanted to live their lives authentically. You will hear stories about how they wanted to stop fighting what they knew deep down. That makes sense. Transition is partially an internal process of alignment. Yet there is also an external component of transition for a lot of people. It does not just end at changing how you think about yourself; usually there is some element of changing your external presentation, or your way of relating to other people in the world. Many people transition to feel in alignment with themselves but also to be seen more accurately by others. This can get confusing when people start to question if they are doing all of this for themselves or for other people. People are afraid to admit there could be any aspect of transition that could be "for other people," because this can feel like it is vanity or caring too much about what other people think. Surely a "real trans person" would transition for themselves and themselves alone?

I don't think so. We exist in community, and we exist in relationships. This is a part of the human experience. It's hard to imagine a person in full isolation. I am sure you have heard the phrase that humans are social animals, and we are. Humans rely on relationships with friends, family, and community for survival. We need the support, protection, and skills of others in order to meet all of the needs of the community and to share the burden of those tasks necessary for survival. This has been true of human beings since our inception and it is no less true of modern humans. We also need social connections for our emotional survival.

Some Western cultures have tried to demand and glorify a life of independence over interdependence to an unreasonable degree, but people always long for connections with others and rely on them. In fact, we are primed for those connections to other human beings from birth. In the first few months of life, a baby's brain is most interested in focusing on the face of the person holding them, and eyes and faces continue to be some of the most interesting stimuli during that time. It is critical to be able to connect to our caregivers when we are unable to do anything for ourselves, and that is why our developing brains prioritize that information so early in life. But that need to connect does not end as we grow older and gain skills to care for ourselves. Being able to connect to and communicate with others is a crucial skillset. Not only does it increase our chances of surviving, but also it increases our chances of thriving. Human connection brings meaning and fulfillment to life.

When it comes to the reasons someone is transitioning, it is impossible to remove other human beings from the equation. We want to be seen, and known, and understood. We want to connect with other people as ourselves rather than as a version of ourselves, or a character. It can feel ironic to want to transition for yourself and also for other people, but I think embracing that can actually be freeing. When you allow yourself to be authentic to yourself and to others, then some of the question of who you are *really* transitioning for is removed. The answer does not have to be a single person.

This is not to say that each individual in your life gets to weigh in on your transition. Not everyone deserves a part in your process. Some people deserve a lot of distance and strong boundaries. This is less about any individual person and more about your ideal relationships with other people generally. What is your ideal relationship with people who have proven to be safe and trustworthy? If you have not met those people yet, what would you imagine it could be? The goal in these questions is to determine what kind of person you would like to be around other people who have proven themselves and who are deserving of your authentic experience. If you have not found those people yet, that is okay, and it is still worth considering what transition means within relationships.

Trans people spend years of their lives role-playing the kind of person they think other people want them to be without knowing it. This means that it can become almost second nature to play one character with your mom and one character at school and one character at work and one character at the grocery store and so on. Even before there is any conscious knowledge that this could be about gender, there is still a strong need to figure out how to navigate relationships safely without letting other people have access to aspects of yourself that could be used against you. This becomes a matter of safety. Protecting yourself from harm relies on knowing what other people want you to be and playing that role convincingly. This is exhausting and it also keeps you separate from people. Initially, the 20-foot high, reinforced steel wall is the goal. If you can't be reached, then you can't be harmed. It is the most basic mechanism of safety. But this eventually becomes a problem when you are open to authentic connections with people and have no idea how to remove this very sturdy wall.

Integrating your identity into a more cohesive sense of self allows those kinds of connections without the constant role-playing. The goal of integration is not to overshare and tell people who do not need to know that you are trans that you are trans. It would be awkward and unnecessary to introduce yourself as trans to the person taking your order at a coffee shop. The goal is to simply allow yourself a range of interactions that are within your actual range, rather than being outside of yourself. Instead of slipping into the role of daughter when you are not a daughter, or slipping into the role of nice young man if you are not a man, instead you will be able to be a person who makes professional small talk over here and a person who has deep conversations over there, all as yourself.

Integration of all the parts of your self is then for yourself and for others, not either/or. More specifically, it is so that you can be yourself around others. This does not have to involve any physical or medical transition, but it can.

Interestingly, I have heard many trans people talk about their desire to physically transition on a deserted island. They believe it would be nice to have all the awkward stages, or the slow progression, far away from the eyes of other people. It actually turns out people do not like that as much as they thought they would. I wrote this book in the first year of the great coronavirus pandemic, and early pandemic was an opportunity for lots of people to have all the isolation they did or did not want. We were all stuck inside with puzzles and streaming services and not a lot else. As I talked to many trans people at various stages of transition, most of them said that they felt like there was something huge missing. They felt like they had absolutely no social feedback around their gender. They did not have any information about how people were reading them or relating to them. While the isolation was a welcome chance not to perform old gender roles or presentations, it was completely devoid of feedback around new experiments. While those who were undergoing medical transition were grateful to have time for the progression of those effects, they also struggled to identify if anything obvious was actually happening according to outsiders. They felt like they could not make necessary adjustments or fine tune their presentation in any way. They could not see themselves through other people's eyes. People felt disconnected and felt like their transition was put on hold in a new and unexpected way.

It turns out trans people are very bad at assessing changes on their own. Dysphoria makes our brain into a fun house mirror. You hyperfocus on features you find upsetting, and they become large and distorted in your mind's eye. It becomes nearly impossible to see past those features. That means when someone goes through the slow process of a hormonal transition, they continue to hyperfocus on those upsetting features and do not notice changes elsewhere. Not to mention that it is extremely hard to notice if anything is happening if you look at yourself in the mirror three dozen times a day to see if anything has happened. Think about when you were a child and you saw some family friend or extended family member who said, "You are getting so tall!" You never noticed getting any taller because it was happening in tiny increments day by day. You could not see it. You never woke up and said, "I'm one sixteenth of an inch taller than I was yesterday!" But for the person who saw you once a year, they could tell immediately that something was different. Physical transition is similar to growing taller or aging in that way; it happens in microscopic increments that build up over weeks and months and years. Without external feedback, you will almost certainly have a really difficult time seeing changes.

Even when acknowledging the usefulness of external feedback and its benefit to identity integration, it can still be extremely scary to feel subjected to the opinions of other people. This is why we cling to our own assessments of progress and shun other people. This is what fuels the deserted island fantasy or the desire to spring out of a cocoon fully formed. The goal is not to go to the other extreme and be desperate for external approval either. There is a balance between being isolated and self-reliant and completely reliant on the approval of others. It is human to accept that we have social and communal needs, and with that we are going to need to have social and communal experiences throughout transition in order to calibrate ourselves to our communities.

The fantasy of complete self-reliance also assumes there is a "true gender" deep down, past the reach of our interactions and relationships. There is no objective, pure, internal self that exists outside of the relationships that form us and help us thrive. We are relational, and our genders are relational too. The goal is then not to try to boil down your gender to its most isolated version. A pure, non-relational gender is a fantasy in the same way that a pure, non-relational personality is a fantasy. Instead, the goal is to assess which relationships are not allowing your gender to present authentically and removing them to the degree that is possible, and filling your life with relationships that allow your ever-changing growth and truth.

CHAPTER 6

Your Gender Doesn't Care What You Think of It

It is extremely unlikely that any of us will ever know the full picture of what has made us who we are. In some ways, life is a mystery novel where we pick up clues along the way, but we can never know every detail of the ancestors whose genetics we share, or the environmental details of our first few months of life, or even how the decisions of a person or corporation on the other side of the world are affecting our day-to-day life. We are a massive collection of the past and present, and we are influenced by the external and internal. This means sometimes our ideas of how things should work based on the evidence we have does not seem to make sense. We look at the information we have about our lives and sometimes it is hard to reconcile what is happening with what we believe should be happening.

It is very common for clients to come to therapy for the first time feeling that they have no reason to be sad, depressed, or struggling to complete the tasks of daily life. They point out all the best parts of their lives as evidence for why the unpleasant feelings don't make sense. They describe how they have a good job or good friends or a good partner or a good place to live or had a good childhood or all of the above. In that case, a therapist will often walk a client through the other parts of their life to see if there is anything unmentioned that is causing distress. Not because the therapist believes the client does not have those good things in their life, but because it is not a full picture and maybe there is important information that can be found in the things that "don't feel like a big deal." And that is very commonly the case. A client feels that their lack of sexual satisfaction with their partner shouldn't be a big deal if their partner is otherwise wonderful, so they try to suppress the feeling. They don't believe their trauma counts as trauma because it is not as big or ongoing as the trauma of someone who has experienced war or famine. They don't believe that their strained relationship with their mom should be a big deal because at least she's sober now, and the relationship is better than it's ever been. They don't consider how their lack of sleep from the construction outside their apartment could be contributing to their irritation and mood, which is influencing their work performance.

Again this is not the therapist's attempt to undermine the client's story, but instead it seeks to add more richness and depth to it. The goal is to take the good with the bad and see what happens when all the pieces are examined together. Everything the client is saying is true, but what they say is not exhaustive and can require some more investigation. This is because it is hard to see the full image when we are missing pieces of the puzzle. As frustrating as puzzles can be, they cannot be solved by smashing pieces where they do not fit.[3]

When it comes to theorizing about ourselves and our genders, sometimes it can be very easy to get caught up in what we think the result should be rather than focusing on the image that is slowly forming in front of us. We get so caught up in the idea of what the picture should be or what we have been told it has to be that we lose sight of what makes much more sense, and we even stop looking at new information as it comes in. As it turns out, discarding information that does not fit our preconceived notions is another thing humans are very good at.[4] And despite the fact that we will never know all of the pieces that contribute to our personal gender identities, that does not mean we can ignore the pieces that feel inconvenient.

One 1989 study has shown that 20 percent of transgender people have served in the US military (which is double the rate of the US population who have served).[5] For trans feminine people, this has been theorized to be due to a "flight into hypermasculinity."[6] A flight into hypermasculinity is pretty much exactly what it sounds like: It is an earnest attempt for someone to prove their masculinity either to themselves or others (or more often, both). Military service is manly, or so goes the cultural narrative. And in a gender crisis, it is common for people to throw themselves into their assigned gender role with an energy that they have not previously attempted. For someone who has been told they just need to *toughen up* or *be a man*, then the military can seem like the right place to see what it is like to do exactly that. In the case of the flight of hypermasculinity, it is usually not long before they realize that the problem was not how much energy they dedicated to the exercise of manliness, it was the manliness. This occurs for trans masculine people as well. There is commonly a last-ditch effort at hyperfemininity before realizing that the problem isn't the effort given to the task; it is that they are attempting the wrong task. Apparently cis people don't find performing their genders a task! Whether fleeing into hypermasculinity or hyperfemininity, trans people find that they cannot convince, cajole, debate, or beg their gender to be something other than what it is.

I believe that your gender does not care what you think of it, and in some ways it exists on its own terms. Your gender is whatever it is without your input or opinion. This is not at all to say that you are held hostage by your gender identity and will be forced to meet its demands. It does not mean that you were born with a gender identity fully formed and untouched by the society around it. Instead, it is something closer to the way your liver does not care what you think of it. You can understand your liver or not; in fact, you can be aware of its existence or not, and it will still be in your body doing its thing. Whether you love or hate or feel ambivalent about your liver, it will still filter toxins from your body. It would be strange to be mad at your liver and wish it was a pancreas, and it would be odd to be disappointed that it did not function like a spleen. There are ways you can support your liver function and there are ways you can make its job a lot more difficult. Yet no matter how hard you wish for it to be something else, it will still be either a supported liver or a struggling liver.

I believe your gender is like a liver in that way. You have a gender identity that may be stifled or supported; it may be understood by you or be far from it, but it exists. Again, of course, there is no way to bring out any sort of medical device and scan the exact shape and measurements of your gender. There is no one outside of yourself who can diagnose it or explain to you what it is or what it looks like. You get to subjectively experience it. This could seem like a downside, but I don't believe it is.

When you subjectively experience your gender, you have the tools and sensors to determine what works for your gender and what does not work for it. Those sensors are your feelings. Say you put a hat on and you say, *Hey, gender, how do you like this hat?* and then you experience a sense of discomfort, dysphoria, or strange nausea. It is probably safe to say your gender is not a fan of the hat. You adjust. Perhaps your gender would like a different kind of hat, a more feminine, masculine, or androgynous one. Perhaps your gender just does not like hats. Not every gender wants to pull off a hat.

Alleviating dysphoria requires addressing your gender on its own terms and not attempting to fight or love it into submission. This is why body positivity does not work to cure or alleviate gender dysphoria, although it is frequently prescribed to do the job. Body positivity allows someone whose body has traditionally been deemed unattractive or inadequate to push back against those societal narratives and say, *Hey, my body is a good body, leave it alone!* This is an individual reclaiming their own experience and creating a new relationship with their body in light of societal pressure.' Body positivity is entirely the wrong tool for the job of alleviating dysphoria, although it can be a great tool for many other jobs.

Some trans theorists have discussed trans brains as having a blueprint for our bodies that end up not being met as we develop. Perhaps these blueprints are general sorts of instructions rather than meticulous lists of features. Perhaps our brains assume traits like our shoulders being wider than our hips or vice versa. Perhaps our brains assume that we will have breasts or no breasts, hair or no hair, external or internal genitals. Other theorists have expanded the metaphor to ask what if your body is like a vehicle that is expecting to run on a certain kind of fuel. What if having testosterone as the dominant hormone in a body that expects estrogen as the dominant hormone is like putting diesel into the engine of a car that takes gasoline? The metaphor is not perfect, and I cannot pretend to know enough about cars to say more.[8] This is simply to say that our bodies may have expectations about the features and shape that they should develop into, and the experience of dysphoria is the space between what is unconsciously expected from the blueprint and what appears instead.

Many assume that there will be no benefit to hormones until there are noticeable physical changes, or perhaps even that there will be no benefit until there are enough noticeable changes to be "passable,"[9] but this frequently is not the case. A significant number of people state that they feel calmer, more energetic, more emotionally connected, and many other positive responses long before any noticeable physical changes occur. A significant number of trans people find that even the first few days or weeks on hormones can have an unmistakable positive mental health effect.

If this benefit is not the result of outward physical changes and the resulting confidence, then it must be the result of something internal. It is then reasonable to think that it may be the way the hormones themselves interact with a trans person's body and brain. In other words, what happens when you put diesel fuel into a diesel engine? The car actually functions! These immediate positive mental health effects are seen in trans people who take testosterone as well as those who take estrogen, so the effect cannot be attributed to a single hormone. If you want me to explain to you why that happens on a biological level, I certainly cannot do that. Researchers are beginning to look into how hormone exposure in utero affects gender development.

Perhaps that is a large piece of the puzzle, or perhaps it is only a very small part. There is only the most basic and preliminary information available on the biological components of gender formation, and due to the complexity of human beings, I will venture to say that even when more information is gathered it will be debated for a long time.

This is simply to say that for many trans people, hormones are the missing piece. Not just because they lead to physical changes that lead to feeling aligned with their sense of self, but also because their brains function more smoothly. Life can become less strained and more effortless. Their bodies can feel calmer. For some trans people, hormones are the way to bring that unconscious blueprint and reality into alignment.

Whether your gender identity can be aided by physical changes or medical transition or not, it is worth considering what may bring you and your gender into alignment without placing too many expectations on what those kinds of changes mean. By not presupposing what your gender is and what it should be okay with, you allow yourself to determine the truth of it. You allow it to tell you when it feels good and when it hurts. You allow it to let you know when it feels supported and when it feels abandoned. Even if your gender does not tell you exactly how it formed into itself, it works hard to tell you what it needs to coexist peacefully with the rest of you. If you can listen carefully to it without assumptions, it will tell you what you need to know.

CHAPTER 7

The Illusion of Responsibility

You have the ability to choose a lot of things when it comes to your transition. Do you want to change your name? Do you want to change your hair? Do you want people to use different pronouns for you? Do you want to shave or stop shaving? Do you want to start hormones? Do you want to have surgery? Do you want to tell your 97-year-old great-aunt? You get to choose the answers to all of those questions, and as we already know, you also get to choose to change your mind.

Trying to figure out the answers to these questions can be hard enough on its own, but unfortunately most of us have also internalized another nefarious narrative that makes it even harder to identify our own desires. We believe that anything negative that may occur after making these decisions is our fault. We have internalized the cis admonishment of, "Well, what did you expect to happen?" So you tell your great-aunt Lalo and she's upset. Your dad tells you if you are going to dress like that, then you should not come to her 98th birthday party. "What did you expect? She's old, she doesn't understand this trans stuff. She grew up in a different time and place; you should have just pretended for a couple more years." It hurts. And the doubt creeps in. *Should I have waited? Was it selfish of me to tell everyone?*

Should I just have white-knuckled it through a couple more family birthday parties and weddings, or maybe every family birthday party and wedding until my dying day?

Obviously, all of that is up to you, but the narrative that makes you think you need to is hypocritical.

Imagine another scenario: You have been diagnosed with cancer; the doctors tell you your best chance at survival is to undergo chemotherapy. While you are most likely terrified and unsure of the future, you learn enough to understand the potential risks and benefits. So you agree to the treatment. While it looks like it is going to be effective, you begin to lose your hair. Part of you thinks it is silly to be upset about your hair when you are dealing with something as big as cancer. Another part of you just misses it and is not soothed by the logic of knowing that this is a small side effect of a life-saving treatment. Your friend comes to visit you in the hospital and you express your sadness about your hair. They say, "That's really stupid. It's just hair; what did you expect to happen?" In this scenario, who is the asshole?

I hope you confidently said it was your friend, because it is your friend in this hypothetical scenario. Just because you agreed to chemotherapy does not mean you are happy with every effect of it. The treatment could be the exact choice you needed to make and feel fully confident having made, and still there are parts that are painful and unpleasant and uncomfortable and inconvenient. If your friends distanced themselves and disappeared during the process of you being ill, no one would tell you, "Well, you shouldn't have been so selfish as to seek treatment." If they did, they would undoubtedly be the asshole.

Yet for whatever reason, when it comes to transition, we are told we are being selfish and we believe them. This chemotherapy example was by no means intended to imply that being trans is a disease or a disorder, and it is certainly not meant to imply that a trans identity is a cancer. (Our goal is not to eradicate transness, but to eradicate the distress of the experience.) This example is simply meant to show that for many trans people, dysphoria has treatment (whether that is medical transition or not) and people frequently get mad at us for seeking that treatment. We begin to believe it is something that we personally need to address. Instead of focusing on how you are attempting to save yourself, you are focused on how other people feel about it. While other people's feeling about transition can be very large and intense, the size of the reaction is not a demand that you must respond to it. You have no more obligation to address it than if someone had a tantrum about you getting contact lenses. Their feelings about it are fully separate from the objective goodness or bad-ness of the decision, and even if their concern is well intentioned, they are still not the person with the necessary information to make the decision. Only you can ever be that person. If some-one decided that they thought wearing glasses was a better fit for your life than contact lenses, or that they just did not trust contact lenses and did not see why you needed them at all, you might respond or you might not, but you certainly would not need to convince them that contact lenses are good and safe and the right decision for you before you started to wear them.

We internalize the cis-centric belief that gender transition is a change that is more extreme than other kinds of change, and that medical transition is more dangerous than other med-ical treatment. This internalization leads to medical transition feeling different from other types of treatment and to a kind of unexplainable guilt that we are doing something to other people by making choices for ourselves. I wouldn't be surprised if your mind is rushing to find ways that those other kinds of medical treatment *are* different than medical transition. If that is the case, then I would suggest taking some time to confront that thought and working out what the difference is to you.

The doors are closing

It is common that transition can feel like a closing door, or in other words, that by making a decision to transition you are closing doors to future possibility. Hormonal transition can often bring this up for people, including one frequent anxiety: Am I closing the door on fertility and having my own biological children? We believe that there is potential, and hormones or surgery could end that potential. Interestingly, many of the trans people I have spoken to about the loss of fertility are not incredibly interested in having biological children in the first place. Of course, some are, and in that case, the options for having biological children should be discussed with a trans-affirming medical provider. But many other trans people are more afraid of the idea that a door is closing than what the actual door leads to or if that was ever a door that they wanted to pass through in the first place. Often the parent of the trans person (or the grandparent of the hypothetical baby) will have been incredibly invested in the idea of grandchildren, and the trans person, early in their process of deciding how to proceed with their own transition, feels incredible guilt for removing that possibility for their parent. I can't tell you how many times I have had this conversation with clients. This dilemma is so difficult because everyone believes the potential exists and it is willfully being rejected, or in other words, it is seen as a conscious or unconscious choice to upset the hypothetical grandparent.

Let's reframe this. What if it is not a conscious choice so much as a side effect of the main treatment? Infertility is not a guaranteed or immediate side effect of hormone therapy, but it can be an eventual effect.[10] For the sake of argument though, let's assume the worst-case scenario, where transitioning does lead to infertility (whether that is due to hormone treatment, surgery, or outdated legal requirements of sterilization in certain countries). Is this the fault of the trans person? Yes and no. It is the result of an action, but in the same way that hair loss is the result of chemotherapy. The choice of chemotherapy is never so simple as, "Do you want your hair to fall out? Yes or no."

This is not to say that people cannot feel sadness and grief around it. Sometimes these choices are extremely difficult. But the narrative states that the trans person made a conscious decision to seek treatment and everything that occurs afterward is something they must be held accountable for as well. Again, "Well, what the hell did you think was going to happen?" What they thought was going to happen is probably that this treatment might make them feel better.

Maybe the chemo example seemed extreme. You thought, *Yeah, but that's serious. If I didn't transition, I wouldn't die*, and maybe that is true. Of course, the suicide rates for trans people are incredibly high, but maybe you are not someone who feels you are suffering so deeply that it would come to that. Still a life of low levels of unease or distress is far from thriving. A life where things just feel vaguely off and uncomfortable for decades is still a burden. You might already be wearing those contact lenses I mentioned, and while you probably would have survived your whole life without them, why would you do that? You do not have to do that, and no one was asking you to. Being able to read street signs and see leaves on trees is probably pretty nice, and probably a lot easier than squinting really hard all day every day. You do not deserve a life that demands strain and headaches if there is an easy way to prevent them.

The reality is you are responsible for either the good and the bad or neither the good nor the bad. You cannot be responsible for the bad and not responsible for the good, although so many people are convinced that this is the case. This realization is very freeing because becoming your authentic self is one of the best things you will ever do. If you hold the good and the bad together, you will find that there are downsides and there can be loss and grief and sadness. But generally those are other people's choices to abandon you in a time where you finally give yourself the gift of your authentic experience. This is entirely different than you doing something to someone else. Which means despite this narrative of personal blame and accountability, many of the downsides are initiated by other people's actions and decisions, rather than your own.

Sometimes people will go so far as to gaslight you and tell you that you are ruining their life, ruining this family, ruining your body, ruining your future, or causing drama. You are not. You both do not have to dissuade them of that and do not have to hold their narrative for yourself. They are allowed to feel that, but it does not make it your responsibility to prevent them from feeling that or take away those upsetting feelings for them.

If you were born a cisgender female and you learned around puberty that you were infertile, you might have incredibly strong feelings of grief. Or maybe not; maybe you would say, "Eh, that's fine, I didn't really see myself having kids anyway." Maybe it would be your mom who would be grief-stricken that her vision for your future was not what she expected, and she would have to entirely re-evaluate what it meant if she could not be a grandmother to a biological grandchild. There are plenty of possibilities surrounding how you and the people around you might feel about this news. But chances are that no one would blame you for your infertility. They would not tell you that this was your fault, and how dare you do this to your mother! Hopefully they would be able to hold your feelings alongside their own. Because of course the reality is that you did not do anything to anyone. And the same is true when you are trans, even when they claim this "choice" was a choice to harm them. You know deep down that it was a choice to live, it was a choice to thrive, it was a choice to continue and survive.

When you make the decision to be the truest and most honest version of yourself, maybe everything else is just what happens alongside it. It is not something you meant to help or harm anyone with; it simply is. Try to hold this thought for as long as you can tolerate it: Perhaps whatever happens is exactly what had to happen.

One more time: *Perhaps whatever happens is exactly what had to happen.*

This can be hard to hold. Your brain might reject it outright. But what if your losses were not your responsibility and they were something you were simply allowed to feel your feelings around?

The other lives you imagined for yourself were a fantasy. What if you take estrogen and in the process of finding the right dose you experience some unpleasant side effects like hot flashes or migraines? Was there a version of life where you did not experience those symptoms? Possibly. Was there a version of life where you experienced no unpleasant effects from the hormones your body naturally produced or the ones you put into it? Absolutely not. Hormones are going to do what hormones are going to do.

What if you take testosterone and you end up with thinning hair that eventually turns to balding? Is that your fault? What about if you had been a cisgender man and you had thinning hair from the testosterone produced within your body? Would you have considered that your fault? The only reason you might consider it your fault in the example of hormone therapy is because you see that taking hormones was a choice you could have not made and therefore you could have been free of hot flashes or hair thinning. The potential is a fantasy, but the potential becomes crystallized in our minds to the point where it seems like a clear pathway for our future, and instead we chose to take a different route. What if that path never existed at all?

Sometimes what trans people are desperately holding on to is the worse option. There is no way to know what comes after the fantasies without taking the steps to find out. I know for a fact that the reality can be so much more beautiful than you might be able to imagine at this time. Right now you can probably think of a time when your fears clouded your vision, and what actually happened was wonderful. Maybe that was moving to a place where you did not know anyone, or ending a relationship, or quitting your job, or dropping out of school. All of those things can be so terrifying because it feels like the bad things that could come after are certain and the good ones are only a naive hope. Allow yourself to ask what would happen if your fears are not your reality but just fears. And what would happen if your hopes are not naive, they are just hopes. It is completely natural to be scared. In fact, it is required, and the amount your mind focuses on your fears is not actually correlated with how likely they are to occur.

PART II

Context and History

Now that you understand more of your own doubt and what to do with it, let's talk more about how it got here. We have briefly discussed some of the context and historical narratives that have led to us internalizing transphobia, but of course there is more to it. Gender and sex are often discussed as if they can be understood through science alone, but is that true? The fields of biology and psychology both have their biases, and those biases have impacted the way trans identities are deemed real or not. How did we get here? Are these questions for psychology or philosophy? Are these the only lenses through which we should look at gender and sex? And if they're not, are they serving us by keeping them?

CHAPTER 8

Sure, Gender Is a Social Construct, but So Is Sex

You have probably heard someone say that gender is a social construct, or that gender is performative. If you have taken a gender studies class in the past 20 years, you may be sick of hearing about it. But for those of you who haven't had to write a paper on them, what do those phrases mean?

When something is a social construct it simply means that its power and meaning are partially based on how a collection of humans view it, or based on how it's viewed in a social capacity. Social constructs can be massive structures, like the ideas of the law, economics, and government. While natural laws like gravity will still function whether you are aware of them or believe in them, social constructs depend on the agreements of people to hold power. If tomorrow everyone decided that the stock market was meaningless, then it would be meaningless, because there is no objective truth in our universe that says the stock market must exist and it must exist exactly as it does today. It could change or disappear entirely without disrupting the function of the natural world.

Gender as a social construct is sometimes harder for people to grasp. Many believe that gender is purely biological and uninfluenced by culture. (Many of these people also equate biological sex and gender.) But gender is deeply influenced by culture, and the ways we culturally discuss gender, gender roles, and gender identity are based on the beliefs of society. We all know that there is nothing inherently masculine or feminine about the color pink. It is just a color. But pink went from being seen as a very masculine color in the 1800s to being seen as a very feminine color in the 1900s. It was once seen as being a lighter shade of the masculine and warlike color red, and then somewhere in the early twentieth century it became a good marketing strategy to have distinct colors for girls' and boys' clothing and the color swapped. Nothing changed about the color itself; it was merely pushed around by the whims of various people. The same is true for larger elements of gender. Our cultural ideas of what makes up a gender, and what is inherent to certain genders, is influenced by many factors. Even the biological factors, which are commonly believed to be facts alone, are subject to interpretation through cultural lenses.

Then we have gender performativity, which is an idea within social constructionism and was made famous by Judith Butler. It claims that ideas of masculinity and femininity are not inherent parts of maleness or femaleness. In other words, having the sex of male does not have a direct correlation to masculine presentation or traits. Masculinity and femininity are learned concepts and therefore learned behaviors. The way we understand masculinity or femininity is in relation to others and in relation to other people's concepts of masculinity and femininity as well. Although it sounds similar, performativity does not mean the kind of performance that takes place on a stage. Performativity is about ways we enact things in the context of our cultures. All the ways that a person walks or talks or the clothes that they wear and the roles that they play are things we define through what is done consistently. Performativity is a repetition of the acts that we then call gender.

These concepts were never intended to be weaponized against trans people. In fact, Judith Butler is completely opposed to their words being used against trans people." But people either misunderstand or intentionally misconstrue these theories to claim that trans identities are fake. People hear the phrase "social construct" and automatically assume that means it is not real. (If you want to go down the road of using social constructionism to claim that things socially constructed are fake, then you are going to end up with a whole lot of fake things. Money is also a social construct, and if you want to argue with a debt collector that money is fake, then, well, I truly wish you the best of luck.)

In an attempt to simplify the complexity of sex and gender, people will sometimes say that sex is biological, and gender is how you think of yourself. (Sometimes people also say that gender is in your head and sex is between your legs, which is even less accurate and pretty crude.) It is understandable to want a quick and pithy sentence to facilitate that *aha!* moment, but oversimplifying it to that degree is almost always harmful to trans and intersex people, and in fact, cis people as well. Whether people want to believe it or not, sex is also a social construct. A person's sex is a combination of genitals, hormones, and chromosomes. Our society tends to focus on genitals almost exclusively, and certainly does so when it comes to assigning gender to newborns. Gender reveals are, of course, actually just genital reveals, and when you are born, the doctor does not do a chromosome test but instead announces your gender based on the presence of a vagina or penis. The vast majority of the time, that is all there is to it, and that goes unquestioned throughout someone's life. It is a flawed system for a number of reasons.

First, even genitals are not a binary. The common belief is that some bodies have penises and some have vaginas and that the internal male and female reproductive systems come along with their respective external genitalia. This is not always the case. External genitalia do not always match the assumed internal reproductive organs. Bodies can and do have countless variations of genitalia expressions and reproductive organs. Even some external genitalia are not clearly a penis or a vagina when a child is a newborn, and those with these tend to be the individuals who are identified as intersex at birth (rather than at puberty or another later date). Throughout history, doctors have made arbitrary distinctions of when a clitoris is considered too long or a penis is considered too short on newborns. There is a window in between these lengths that has been considered medically unacceptable and this is when doctors have either suggested surgery or gone ahead and performed surgery without even the consent of a parent. While there are rare cases when a newborn needs immediate surgery on their genitals in order to urinate (or due to other medical concerns), far more often there is no functional concern and the decision is simply a doctor's personal belief of what the newborn's genitals should look like. These unnecessary surgeries on intersex children can lead to scarring, infections, loss of reproductive ability, loss of erotic response, and many other side effects. Clear harm has been done in the name of what is considered "normal"—a primarily aesthetic normality. Thankfully, with the help of a great deal of work by intersex advocates, those surgeries are occurring less and less frequently, but this is a fight that is far from over. It has taken a great deal of work to make the medical field acknowledge that they were performing unnecessary and dangerous surgeries due to their own beliefs of what a body should look like.

So society's favorite determiner of sex—genitals—are not a binary, and sex chromosomes are not a binary either. In school we learned that XX chromosomes mean you are a girl, and XY chromosomes mean you are a boy. What it really means is that those chromosomes determine certain aspects of your body and development. Much like the supposed binary nature of genitals, XX and XY are not the only combination of sex chromosomes that are possible. It is possible to have XXY, XXXY, XYY, XO (where O indicates an X or Y chromosome has been lost), and more. Unless there is a medical concern, people do not get their chromosomes verified. Unambiguous genitals at birth, and a puberty that goes according to expectations, is enough assurance to not investigate someone's sex chromosomes any further. If you were to ask random people which sex chromosomes they have, you would either get people telling you they did not know or an answer like "Well, I'm a woman, so they're XX." This is not a verified fact but an assumption based on what we know to be statistically common. It is rare to find someone who knows the answer based on chromosome analysis. For the vast majority of people, if they ever think of their chromosomes at all, they are going to assume they are with another supposed binary.

Hormones are the least binary of all the determiners of sex. While testosterone and estrogen are the two primary hormones people tend to think about when they think of sex hormones, there are many others. Androgens—which include testosterone and dihydrotestosterone (DHT)—and estrogens—which include estradiol and progesterone—are simply two broad categories of steroids. Previously, androgens were considered the "male hormones" and estrogens were considered the "female hormones" because of the strong belief in their primary importance in their respective sexes. This has been found to be an extreme oversimplification, and all sexes and genders are impacted by the effects of androgens and estrogens. These hormones not only influence development, libido, and reproduction but also affect the brain, bones, heart, and liver, to name a few. Hormones also do not stay at fixed levels throughout the lifespan. Most people know that hormone levels in cisgender women shift throughout the menstrual cycle, and menopause is a more drastic change in hormone production later in life. But cisgender men undergo similar changes in hormone levels throughout their lifespan, and what has been dubbed "andropause" is the experience of declining production of androgens. What is considered the "normal ranges" of these hormones is wide, and it is not always obvious where to place the delineations of when a hormone is considered too high or too low. This can show up in medical settings, but it also shows up when binaries are enforced in settings like professional sports.[12]

Instead of any single aspect of our sex being a binary, they all essentially exist as sometimes shifting (hormones) and sometimes stagnant (sex chromosomes) locations on a non-binary scale. Society has reduced sex to obvious features and not allowed them to have the nuance and fluidity that these biological traits actually do have. It is a common refrain online that a person cannot argue their biological sex. Sometimes these trolls are generous enough to allow for what they consider the delusion of gender identity, but most of the time they are not so generous. They believe that a penis comes along with testes and a prostate, XY chromosomes, and a testosterone-dominant body, and all of that equals a male sex. While that is a common body, it is not one of two types of body. And the presence of a penis does not necessitate all the other pieces, even before we get to gender identity. But this is not just an annoying misunderstanding that leads to annoying internet debates; these ideas also create false binaries within legal and even medical documentation.

The purpose of this chapter is not to get into the minutiae of social constructionism or to debate its finer points, and it is not even to go into depth on the biology of sex. If that is what you are looking for, there are plenty of texts that get into that and hopefully be as science- or theory-heavy as you want them to be.[13] The purpose is simply to break down yet another narrative that states that a person's sex is objective and real and that their gender is subjective and fake. That kind of narrative is usually just a gentler form of transphobia, where a person can claim to support trans identities but also not fully believe they are valid and deserving of respect. Maybe this is the scientific version of "love the sinner, hate the sin."

Not only are scientists gathering more information about the human body and brain daily, but there is certainly an interplay between sex and gender that is not yet understood. It would be impossible for one of these to be purely objective while the other is purely subjective. I suspect that gender is the subjective experience of how we experience our biological sex, combined with other factors like environment, culture, and personal life experience. And while some of that is a question for science, some of that is a philosophical question, which is what makes discussing gender such a mess. Most people are not ready to consider that gender could exist at all in the realm of philosophy.

Even if you were to claim that a person's gender is their subjective and personal interpretation of their biology (which I would say is missing quite a few pieces of the puzzle), then you still end up in the realm of philosophy. And once you are in philosophy land, you end up with new messy questions like: How do we talk about an experience like gender dysphoria? How do we categorize it? Do we categorize it at all? Is it a diagnosis?

Thankfully these are not all questions that need to be answered before you decide what to do about your own gender (or ever!) but let us play with them for just a few more minutes.

CHAPTER 9

Some Historical Context and the DSM

For the sake of argument, let us assume you think it is a worthwhile endeavor to make gender dysphoria a diagnosis. Where do you begin? It's a difficult thing to pull off because gender dysphoria is neither purely physical nor purely mental. As I have mentioned, it can't be diagnosed through traditional medical means like blood tests, brain scans, diagnostic surgery, or other traditional medical assessments. One alternative method of diagnosis would be to assess it in the same way you assess a mental illness. This is what the DSM has attempted to do.

For some background, the DSM, or the *Diagnostic and Statistical Manual of Mental Disorders*, was first created in 1952 by the American Psychiatric Association (APA). It has gone through multiple editions and revisions, and in 2022 the DSM is on its fifth edition. It was originally intended to solve the problem of multiple classification systems that existed at the time and to create a common language in psychiatry. The first two editions relied primarily on prose descriptions of different diagnoses. The third edition created much more defined diagnostic criteria, which was missing from the first two. That was intended to create more clarity and specificity in the diagnostic process, and it was also an attempt to bring psychiatry back to its more medical roots.

The first two editions did not include anything specific to gender identity, although homosexuality was included as a diagnosis. The homosexuality diagnosis underwent a few changes before it was removed from the DSM completely in the third edition. The DSM-III was also the first time gender identity disorder was included. Some have argued that this inclusion was a roundabout way of replacing homosexuality, while others believe that the removal of homosexuality and the inclusion of gender identity disorder were unrelated to one another. There is evidence that both of these changes occurred for separate reasons, but perhaps that is a matter of interpretation.

Gender identity disorder was in the DSM-III and DSM-IV until it was changed to the diagnosis of gender dysphoria in the DSM-5 (they also stopped using Roman numerals). The shift intended to reduce stigma, and whether it was successful is heavily debated.

While the DSM claims to be solely based on research, there is no arguing that social pressure and protests have affected change in the book. The diagnosis of homosexuality was one such diagnosis, and the American Psychiatric Association was forced to define what constituted a mental illness as gay activists protested and brought their concerns to the APA. There has been similar social pressure and debates around the continued inclusion of some form of a gender dysphoria diagnosis in the DSM. The DSM is, of course, a book of mental disorders, which begs the question of if it is even possible for inclusion in the DSM not to carry stigma. The move from gender identity disorder to gender dysphoria included diagnostic changes, but that did not necessarily change public perception of being included in a classification of mental disorders, no matter what the specific language within the diagnosis says.

One option would to be remove the diagnosis from the DSM, but that can cause its own issues. The removal of the homosexuality diagnosis did not affect whether gay people could receive therapeutic or medical care, although the same would not be true for gender dysphoria given the current system of medical insurance in countries like the US. The requirement of having a diagnosis to access medical transition has complicated how to proceed.

Another option is to simply have a diagnosis in the ICD (International Statistical Classification of Diseases and Related Health Problems). The ICD has also undergone many revisions, and as of January 2022 it is in its eleventh edition. It has changed from a diagnosis of "transsexualism" to "gender incongruence," and the ICD has moved the diagnosis out of the section for mental and behavioral disorders. Many see this is as a move in the right direction and something that is making a DSM diagnosis redundant. Gender incongruence, as it is called in the ICD, does not carry the same stigma of pathology that inclusion in the DSM carries, because the ICD includes a wide spectrum of diagnostic codes that are not all considered pathology. For example, a diagnosis of pregnancy is included in the ICD, and that is not a diagnosis that means the patient is sick. Replacing the DSM diagnosis of gender dysphoria with the ICD diagnosis of gender incongruence would still allow for the required diagnostic code so that patients can access gender-affirming care through their insurance, and perhaps might also make some small effort to de-pathologize a diagnosis around gender. But, of course, it also allows the required diagnostic code so that patients can have access to gender-affirming care through their insurance.

A diagnosis of desire

For now, the DSM diagnosis now stands as the key to unlocking gender-affirming care for most trans people, which means the language of the diagnosis is not insignificant. The way it's worded impacts who has access to care and who is deemed not clinically trans enough.

When the diagnosis was gender identity disorder in the DSM-IV, the language was primarily around distress. Each part required that the patient was unhappy and wanted to transition due to that deep unhappiness. You saw words like discomfort, disturbance, and distress over and over again.

The entire section on gender identity in the DSM-IV was full of strange language and didn't make a good show of pretending to not be blatantly transphobic. It was extremely hard to have any faith that it had the best interest of trans people at heart.

For example, the section about children called AFAB children girls and AMAB children boys, already working to dismiss trans children from the start. The diagnosis seemingly didn't care if the children were trans or not, and the authors decided to misgender (some of) them anyway. At best this conflated trans children with children who are going through a phase, and at worst, it was just blatant transphobia. After that, the diagnostic features jump in to pop culture references. When discussing trans children's interests, it mentioned Barbie, Batman, and Superman by name. They said a trans girl[14] may have traditionally feminine interests like Barbies and trans boys[15] may have traditionally masculine interests like superheroes.

The addition of these cultural references gave an incredible amount of power to what society has deemed masculine and feminine. Why are Batman, Superman, and Barbie important to a clinical diagnosis? Do these cultural creations mean something inherent about a person's inner being? Do DC Comics and Mattel know that they have this power? Would a child who has never been introduced to these characters be subjected to different standards? Do they matter more than what a child says about themselves?

The description also said that trans boys are sometimes "misidentified" by strangers as boys. Misidentified! This goes back to looking like blatant transphobia. Not only that, but it also gave weight to the opinions of complete strangers off the street before it gave it to the children themselves.

When you look at the full picture of the diagnosis of gender identity disorder, you see that it gave credence to the clinician, the culture, and, in the case of children, absolute strangers before it took into consideration what a trans person says about themselves.

The language in the gender dysphoria diagnosis in the DSM-5 is more respectful, but is far from fixing all of the issues of earlier diagnoses.

For whatever reason they took out Batman and Superman but still mention Barbie by her legal name. There is a lot of discussion about how many children persist in their gender dysphoria from childhood to adulthood,[16] so it seems like the authors excuse themselves from having to actually call these children trans boys and trans girls and instead they switch to saying "natal boys" and "natal girls." It's a weak attempt to acknowledge that, yes, some of these children with gender dysphoria are actually transgender, without acknowledging that there is any flaw in the diagnosis.

The diagnostic criteria themselves use the word "desire" over and over again. The diagnosis is all about wanting to be treated as a different gender, wanting to be another gender, wanting the physical features of a different gender, wanting to be rid of the features of the assigned gender, and so on. Both the old and current versions of the diagnosis say there must be "incongruence," which, in this case, is just a fancy word for a person's gender feeling wrong.

From a brief glance at the current diagnostic criteria, it looks like the diagnoses have changed from focusing primarily on distress to focusing on desire. The language consistently says "strong desire" and "strong conviction" in the DSM-5 instead of the words around distress and disturbance. But then it goes on to say in the diagnostic features that the distress is still required. It begins to look like the DSM is saying that distress and desire are two sides of the same coin. Or in other words, that a trans person will be so unhappy that their desire for changes must be incredibly strong. I suspect the shift in language is an attempt to make the new diagnosis look more like it validates the self-determination of trans people, without letting go of the ultimate power of the gatekeeper. By focusing on desire, it seems to validate the feelings and needs of the patient. But ultimately it says, *This is about what you want, and this doesn't have to be a bad thing, but actually you still need to perform distress, and most importantly you have to perform your need for us as the gatekeepers.*

As we have discussed previously, this works because if you

weren't distressed going in, you will become that way if you're kept from care. They create what they want to see.

Whether you frame it as distress or desire, the DSM by its nature requires that someone else must authenticate your feelings as valid. That is the power of the DSM. We can look at all of the language of these diagnoses and see that they are extremely subjective. We have clinicians determining if the strength of your feeling is correct. Are you sad enough to be clinically sad? Do you desire hard enough to have clinical levels of desire? Is your incongruence incongruent enough? This does nothing except send the message that other people's assessments of your gender are more important than your own.

I'm sure some of you are thinking, *Okay, but the person giving me the diagnosis is a trained professional and not a random stranger.* And yes, they are professionals in that they have degrees and licenses in (mental) health care, but no, that does not mean that they are trained. Most doctors and mental health clinicians have a laughably small educational requirement in LGBT-specific health, if they have a requirement at all. There is no expectation that professionals will have specific knowledge and training around gender identity before they assess for this diagnosis. They are simply a person who gets to decide if your feeling is a strong feeling.

We must then ask: With this level of clinical subjectivity, is this science anymore? Whether you base the diagnosis around distress or desire, it doesn't matter. It takes a person's subjective, internal felt sense and puts it up to a vote by an outsider. Ostensibly the point of a diagnosis is to make sure that the right people access care rather than people who don't truly need it. Or in other words, this intends to address the concern that many people seem to have, which is that you could just walk up to a surgeon and ask for gender-affirming surgery and they would be forced to provide it for you. Instead, they say you must go through the proper channels and be assessed properly. And yet, these are the proper channels. After examining the proper channels, we can see that they consist of someone going, *Yeah, bro, they got a real strong feeling! Give them the surgery.* It's not you making that call; it is someone else. Diagnostically speaking, it must be someone else. The DSM requires that in order to exist.

But a "perfect" system isn't possible. It's not possible to create a system that only allows people who will have zero regrets through and will stop 100 percent of people who will have regrets at the door. The experience of being trans does not fit into a diagnosis because there is no medical or mental health assessment that makes sense. Again these diagnoses can only attempt to assess someone's subjective, internal felt sense. Gender identity is not a disorder, and claiming gender dysphoria is a disorder rather than the identity itself doesn't change anything if the system remains the same. Treating gender or gender dysphoria like a disorder only creates an illusion of certainty that only the correct people will get care, and that the clinician will be safe from the liability of someone regretting their decisions. It does nothing else.

PART III

Mental Health

By now you're probably starting to think that the system is a little (or a lot) broken and it doesn't need to be this way. Hopefully you're starting to realize that the doubts you have are not because you are broken or flawed but because you are intentionally being made to feel that way. This knowledge can be freeing but also exhausting and overwhelming. Being trans is certainly not easy, and there is a lot of pressure on you to manage your mental health on your own. This next section is going to address your mental health and what you're likely feeling during this time. We will discuss the mental health effects of not feeling trans enough as well as the emotional rollercoaster of early transition and beginning to accept the reality of your identity. Then we will talk about how to start addressing that.

CHAPTER 10

Things Could Get Worse Before They Get Better, and That Doesn't Necessarily Mean You're Cis

Without someone else being able to come in and accurately assess your gender, how do you proceed with all the uncertainty? It is up to you to determine your own needs, but that is far easier said than done. Many people who are questioning their gender identity desperately long for an epiphany or a sudden *aha!* moment. There is so much doubt that they hope if they finally build up the courage to actually try whatever it is they have been thinking about for months, then maybe it will all become clear at once. Sometimes that happens for people, but epiphanies, at least how we imagine them, are generally rare and hard to come by, and sometimes realizations bring new questions. It is not uncommon to feel even more confused after proceeding with early aspects of transition.

This can happen for binary and nonbinary trans people and

make them think that they were wrong and maybe they are actually cisgender after all. Again, if you have been endlessly obsessing about gender, it is pretty unlikely that you are cis, but let's take a look at why this happens and what makes it so confusing.

In social transition, this can look like the mixed feelings that occur when people use your new name, pronouns, or titles. You have finally made the terrifying request that people call you something different than before, and then they do. That is great! Right? Then why does it feel so weird? Well first, it feels weird because it sounds weird, and it sounds weird because it is new. You have been responding to one set of pronouns and one name for decades. For a while you will not even realize people are referring to you when they use the new name or pronouns. You are suddenly that person at the coffee shop daydreaming while they call out, "Lily! Lily? ... Lily?" and you're like, *Oh shit, that's me!* This will be an adjustment for anyone, but if you are a people pleaser, you may have the added difficulty of feeling as if you are a fraud or as if you are tricking people. This is because you may interpret your brain's lack of response at the new name/pronouns as a negative sign. Your brain might say, *Hey, uh, that felt weird, something is not right.* And if you do not confront your brain and say, *Yeah, of course it felt weird, I've had a new name for six weeks, it's a tough habit to break,* then your brain just sends out the generic panic response. There are red flashing lights and some siren sounding and you don't know why it is going off, so better safe than sorry. You have to assume there's an emergency, right? Because it feels wrong in some unidentifiable way, you assume you have done something wrong. You feel that you have deceived people. It is a lie, but it is a convincing one.

The panic response is only signaling discomfort, and you have the ability to interpret it as a reaction to a new experience rather than as a signal that you are not trans. Every trans person also goes through a stage of misgendering themselves in their own minds too. It is just what happens when you have talked about yourself in a different way for many years. This is normal, and some level of discomfort around the new experiences is something all trans people go through.

But this is far from the desired epiphany everyone wants, and worse still, many people's dysphoria increases instead of decreasing during this stage. That is because you have gone from a place where you have compartmentalized and maybe even dissociated[17] around your feelings about someone calling you by your old pronouns to suddenly paying attention. Paying attention, and in fact being hyperattuned to these signals, is an extreme level of input where you were previously shut down. Paying attention means you are scrutinizing your experience with the hope and expectation that it will feel so much better than before. That is a lot of pressure. And as stated before, it is just going to be weird because it is new, not necessarily because it is bad or wrong. It must first feel weird before it can feel neutral or positive. In fact, the stage where it feels weird but good is a good sign that you are on a path to discovering what happens after that initial stage of novelty.

Feeling that things are getting worse before they get better can also extend to medical transition. People often start hormones with those same hopes and expectations, and then they panic when their dysphoria intensifies. This can happen for all the same reasons as with social transition: The shift from dissociation to scrutiny is intense, and a new experience is always strange and hard to identify. Managing the experience of consistent dysphoria and living your day-to-day life requires coping mechanisms. It would be nearly impossible to experience dysphoria every second of every day while also managing school or work or home life. Dissociation can work great to create enough distance to allow you to move functionally through the world. This can be another reason that people do not believe they have experienced dysphoria—they get so good at disconnecting from the feeling out of necessity.

But something else can also happen with medical transition, particularly hormonal transition. For many people on hormones, there is a stage where they feel as if the secondary sex characteristics of their first puberty clash with the secondary sex characteristics developing with their second puberty. For someone on testosterone, they might feel like growing hair on their chest while they still have breast tissue is odd, overwhelming, or even disgusting. Or for someone who is taking estrogen, they might find that sprouting breast buds while having a torso that feels like a more masculine or angular shape is also strange, uncomfortable, or upsetting. This is perfectly normal, and even common. Depending on how someone identifies, this may feel like an "in-between" experience of genders, or it may just feel like not how someone imagined their results. This frequently leads to that *I've made a horrible mistake* feeling, especially when it comes to reactions as strong as disgust.

As you can see from the definitely-not-scientific graph of dysphoria below, once people start the process of hormone therapy, they expect their dysphoria to consistently decrease over time. But as we've discussed, the dysphoria can get worse before it gets better, and as it climbs and climbs and climbs there is no one to tell you if or when it will stop increasing. This is when a number of people panic and stop taking hormones. They abandon the process before experiencing the relief.

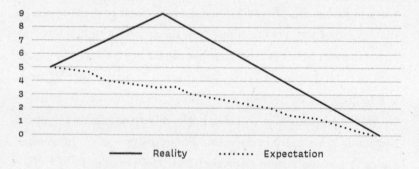

Definitely not a scientific graph of dysphoria

It takes years to experience some of the full effects of hormones. They create some changes very quickly, and others very slowly, when of course many people would prefer they show up all together. Changes in muscle mass and fat redistribution are a few of the changes that take the longest to complete. But unfortunately, those changes in muscle mass and fat redistribution are exactly what can allow other changes, such as breast growth (with the use of estrogen) or body hair growth (with the use of testosterone), to feel aligned on someone's body. In other words, many trans people find it strange or unnerving to have breast development on a torso that still has features they deem masculine, or to have hair growth on a body that they deem feminine. This can be another panic point. How do you determine if you are a person who needs to be on hormones longer in order to experience the positive effects or if you are a person who should stop taking them?

One way that can be helpful to determine if this is your

situation is by asking yourself: If you had a magic wand and could change your appearance instantaneously, what would you change? Does any of it look like what could be expected by continued time on hormones? Does any of it look like more changes in that direction? Does any of it look like fast forwarding or jumping ahead? Of course, your magic wand changes may also include things that hormones will not touch (like height or changes in bone structure), but if some of them are what five to ten years of hormones could provide you, then some of your discomfort can be attributed to this awkward stage and not that hormone therapy is wrong for you.

Almost everyone, no matter how confident in their decision to transition, gets hung up on the idea of "permanent changes." Surgeries are certainly included in that category, but some hormonal changes also can be permanent and therefore terror inducing. The idea of permanent changes can elicit the "closing door" phenomenon we discussed earlier, and it can also bring up many other fears.

The first thing worth mentioning is that no permanent changes occur immediately on hormones. Some of the permanent changes on estrogen are breast growth and eventual decrease or loss of fertility. On testosterone, there is voice deepening and genital growth. None of these occur right away. Voice deepening and genital growth on testosterone can both begin relatively quickly (sometimes in the first few weeks), but they happen in stages over time and certainly do not complete their full effect for months or years. Breast growth on estrogen can also begin within the first few weeks of hormones (although usually there is not a noticeable difference until after the first month). It will also not be completed for months or years.

Many people fear that they will not have enough time

to change their mind and stop hormones if it turns out they actually do not like the effects of hormones. This is certainly worth thinking about and taking seriously, but it is also worth specifically considering the changes that will not revert. That is to say, do not let your brain sound the alarm just at the phrase "permanent changes" without specifying which ones and then thinking about them individually. If you start testosterone, how do you feel about your voice deepening? If you decided to stop testosterone after a few months when your voice has deepened slightly, would you be upset about having that slightly deeper voice? If your answer is no, then you have more time to decide than you may have previously thought. If you start estrogen and you worry about breast growth first, look into how that kind of change actually occurs. When people talk about breast growth beginning in the first few weeks, they definitely do not mean that anyone has noticeable breasts after a few weeks. It generally starts with nipple sensitivity, then what many people describe as a puffiness, which then progresses into what most people think about when they think about breast growth. It takes time. You may receive a lot more information about yourself than you expect around the nipple sensitivity stage.[18]

And while no one wants to think about this, I believe it is worth looking directly at your worst-case scenario. If your worst-case scenario is breast growth and then you discover you hate having breasts, then you can have surgery to remove them. It is not a convenient option, and it is often not a cheap option, but it is an option. At least for now, allow yourself to mentally hold all the options. It is useful to break your options down into easy options and extreme options and all the ones in between and acknowledge that even extreme options are options. Even if you had to fundraise/take out a loan/put the cost on a medical credit card, even if people thought you were weird or you were doing transition wrong, even if you felt a lot of embarrassment or shame, it could still be an option. Do not let your brain decide that because it feels extreme it is an impossibility. Allow yourself to truly assess your range of options from the simplest to what feels the most extreme without taking anything off the list. Because for now, it is simply a list of possibilities.

The fear of detransition[19] is real. Many trans people feel the need to thoroughly research and watch the stories of people who detransition to compare their experiences against these people and check for similarities and differences. This is understandable, but statistically detransition is very rare. Data from the US Trans Survey shows that most people who detransition do so temporarily due to pressure from outside parties (like parents, friends, family members, and/or employers) or because the experience of transitioning was too difficult given their current location or circumstances. Only 5 percent of people who detransition say they did so because they felt they were not trans or transition wasn't right for them. And 5 percent of the people who stated that they detransitioned is 0.4 percent of the total number of those people surveyed. Meaning 99.6 percent of people who had begun a transition process either felt that transition was right for them or that they would need another setting in order to transition safely. Numbers around surgery regrets show similarly low numbers. One study[20] that looked at data spanning from 1972 to 2015 and reviewed 6793 people who sought care through a gender clinic in Amsterdam showed that 0.6 percent of trans women and 0.3 percent of trans men had regrets around gonadectomy.[21]

What is much more common than regret around having surgery at all is that people wish that their surgeries had been done differently, wish that their results were more aesthetically pleasing or more functional, or wish that they had chosen a different surgeon.

Detransition does occur but in rare circumstances. These stories tend to receive more publicity than the prevalence rates demonstrate. Unsurprisingly, these uncommon stories can be used to bolster anti-trans sentiments, and there have been a number of people who detransitioned who do not feel comfortable with the way their story has been used in the media.

And it is totally fine if you are a person who detransitions. There is a great deal of stigma around detransitioning, and there does not need to be. As we have discussed and will continue to discuss, there will never be a way to flawlessly determine who is the perfect candidate for transition without removing a person's agency. There will never be a perfect system of outside gatekeepers who will correctly determine who is really trans and who is not, so that requires that individuals are able to explore this possibility for themselves and determine what they need. Detransition simply means that someone has taken the best available data they had about themselves at the time and has gained more data that has required a change in direction. There is nothing shameful about that.

What is far more common than this cis-to-trans-to-cis detransition story is that many people, in the process of exploring their gender identity, realize that their gender identity is more complex than they had previously anticipated. It is not uncommon for people to go from identifying as a binary trans person to a nonbinary trans person (just as the reverse is not uncommon). Others go from wanting hormonal treatment and all of the surgeries to realizing there are some (or all of the) parts of a medical transition that they are uninterested in. When we remove the narrative that there is only one way to transition, then it becomes impossible to do it correctly or incorrectly. It becomes impossible to fail at it. A person changing their path or direction does not need to be seen as regressing.

I am not discussing these possibilities to scare you. Even asking you to consider the worst possible scenario is not an attempt to create new anxieties you had not even considered yet. It is so that you are prepared to deal with the mental spiraling that occurs with uncertainty. What commonly happens is someone endlessly considers transitioning, and as they tentatively allow themselves to get closer to it their mind hits the brakes and says, *What if something goes wrong and I hate it?* When that occurs, they tend to panic and push all the feelings back into the deep, dark closet they escaped from, and they never actually address that fear. I am asking you to stop that cycle and address it. You will not know all the answers by standing in the doorway between what you know and what you do not know. It may not stop after the first step, or the second. This process can feel like moving through a deep fog and only being able to see an arm's length in front of your face. In order to see more, you must keep walking in a direction. There is no knowing if the direction is the right direction until you are able to stand in that new place and assess it.

Ironically, looking at your worst-case scenario can sometimes be the most useful thing you can do for yourself. Look directly at it and decide if the worst-case scenario seems likely based on what you want and hope and how hormones affect people.

Decide if your worst-case scenario is something that can be "fixed," and if your worst-case scenario is worse than what you are experiencing now. If your worst-case scenario is detransition, then look directly at it.

If you are searching this book for answers, then the fact is that something is not working for you now and you owe it to yourself to acknowledge this and address it. Only time will tell what will come, but you owe yourself the chance to recognize the full extent of your pain, the full extent of your longing, and the full extent of your hope.

Hope is perhaps the scariest feeling of them all. This might seem ironic or counterintuitive, but sometimes it feels more overwhelming to consider the possibility that these are changes that you do want to pursue than it is to consider that maybe transition is not the answer. The reason it can feel so dangerous is because for many people admitting hope and desire and longing means no longer being able to compartmentalize all the feelings. In order to protect yourself you convince yourself that the thing you want is not actually important or a big deal. If you convince yourself that you do not actually want to start hormones or change your presentation, then you can convince yourself that you are not feeling the pain of not having it yet. By pursuing something, you must admit that you want it, and admitting that you want it means admitting that you do not have it, and admitting that you do not have it means admitting that there is a sadness or a pain. That early spike in dysphoria is what happens when you acknowledge the desire for something different without yet having it. Before those feelings were attributed to gender, they could just be a mysterious low mood that had no obvious significance. By admitting to yourself that you want something different, the floodgates of feelings will open, and it is important to know that that is normal and it will not last forever. It is a sign that you are headed in the right direction. You have accessed your grief.

CHAPTER 11

Grief and How to Feel Your Feelings

G rief is a bastard, but unfortunately it is one of the first things we have to address when it comes to trans mental health. While grief is a human experience and one that no one enjoys, it is one that demands the attention of all trans people.

No matter how young you realize your gender identity, unless you are cisgender, you will not have got an entire life where that identity was seen or celebrated. Whether you knew you were hiding your identity or not, there was a time when you did not get to embrace your gender fully, and there is a grief and mourning process that comes along with that.

A lot of people believe that the grief of being trans is about grieving who you used to be before you came out—saying goodbye to the girl or boy you might have thought you were. Some trans people do experience that specific grief, but many do not. Due to dissociation and disconnection, a lot of trans people look back on their pasts and do not recognize anyone to miss or to be sad to lose. The past self is hard to recognize. It looks buried beneath a pile of (effective or ineffective) coping mechanisms. Instead, they think back to all the times they wish they could have built a pinewood derby car but were told that was only for

Boy Scouts, or the time they wished they could have worn the dress to their first day of kindergarten but their parents told them they had to wear something else, or the times when they were a bit older and were told they could not wear eyeliner out of the house. In other words, the grief is not for the person you were before but the person you were not before. For all the things you could not do or be. For all the opportunities you missed and did not have the chance to experience as your true self.

Like every other feeling, trans people try to intellectualize[22] this emotional experience away. You tell yourself that you had it easier than other trans people and you have no right to grieve. *At least you were able to come out at all! At least your family did not disown you! At least you were not attacked or killed!* All of those things can be true and you can be grateful for them, and those truths will do nothing to make the grief go away. The grief will follow you until you feel it.

Intellectualizing is common. Emotions can feel like they are getting in the way of logic and rationality. It can feel like the best option is to figure out how to turn off the feelings, because the feelings serve no purpose. Often we respond to our pain with, *Well, there's nothing I can do about that now, so there's no point having a feeling about it.* Unfortunately, that is not how humans function. Feelings do serve a purpose and repressing them will not make them disappear.

Most of us keep trying to avoid the feelings, and this can become habitual and hard to escape. We become skilled at staying away from the memories that evoke heavy feelings. It never seems like the right time to engage with the pain, and again it can feel pointless to do so. Which means even when we feel ready to engage with emotions, doing so can be difficult because we have previously spent so much time evading and repressing. Many people find that their feelings finally break the surface as they remember childhood memories, but why is that?

Have you ever watched a cartoon that you used to watch when you were a kid and been hit with some overwhelming feeling or sensation or memory you had not had in years? Have you ever smelled something that reminded you of the smell of gluing macaroni to popsicle sticks when you were four years old and suddenly been inundated with memories you did not even know you were storing? Some of our memories are so infrequently accessed that we believe we are no longer storing them, and these sensations can access a route in our minds that something like the instruction to "think about your preschool classroom" would not. These shortcuts and back alleyways of memory seem to bypass the process of adult intellectualization. Adults not only intellectualize feelings but they can also get good at convincing themselves that they deserve the bad things that happen to them. Or they think, *Hey, life is not fair so there's no point in crying about it.* Yet when you were a very small child you just felt your feelings because you did not know how to do anything else. Somewhere along the way we figured out that there was a time and a place to express those feelings, and supposedly it was not on the floor in the middle of a grocery store aisle. But even as adults there are times when we need to be able to tap into those big feelings that we were much more proficient at feeling when we were young. You know on some deeper level that you did not deserve the bad things that happened to you, and you know that some adult telling you that life was not fair was not going to stop your crying. Childhood memories bring back a place before you were taught that you needed to repress your emotions, and reconnecting with that more freely emotive self is intense.

The problem with so-called "negative emotions" is that nobody wants to make time and space to feel them. Your body is like, *Hey, so when do we schedule these 25 years of built up trans grief?* And you laugh and laugh and you do not respond to your body's messages. Your body becomes increasingly annoyed at being ignored and starts to up the ante. This then comes out sideways and you might find yourself irritable, or even angry, at trans people who came out younger than you. *How dare these kids who are able to go on hormone blockers. How dare these young adults whose parents support them enough to make cute and affirming social media videos with them.* Of course, there is no reason to be mad at another trans person, but because you have not processed your grief you decide that for some reason this person has done something to you. This other trans person is having an experience you were not able to have and it feels personal. These are not rational thoughts, and you know it, but it might be extremely difficult to make the feeling go away until you address the real underlying cause, which is the unprocessed grief.

Grief feels unwieldy because it is not a singular emotion; it is a process. There are a lot of ideas about the correct way to grieve, and those can differ across cultures. Many people have taken the five stages of grief[23] as the guidebook to grief. They believe that you must experience denial, anger, bargaining, depression, and, finally, acceptance, and you have to do so in that order. This is not necessarily the case for everyone and if you do experience all of these stages, you certainly will not do so in a linear fashion. Sometimes you are feeling like you finally got all the anger out and you are well on your way to acceptance when all of a sudden the anger is back. That is not wrong, and it is not a regression, it likely just means there is more to process. It is also possible that those five stages are not your experience at all. That is okay too.

If this is a process, then how do you navigate through something so tumultuous and non-linear? Here is where I say the therapist's advice of *feel your feelings*. Stay with me; I promise this is not actually as useless advice as it sounds. In order to get the benefits of feeling your feelings, you might need some help on what feeling them actually means and what it looks like.

The first step is not to shut down feelings as they arise. Often people start to emotionally experience something and shut it down before it even presents itself fully. Perhaps you notice sadness about how you were not able to go to your prom in the clothes you wanted and with a date of the gender you were attracted to, and you think, *That is dumb, at least I got to go to prom at all. Kim, there's people that are dying!* You have barely had a chance to even feel the sadness at all before you are doing the work of trying to logic it away. Intellectualizing your feelings has become a habit. So how do you stay with the feeling and experience it?

You bring yourself back to it. When your brain tells you that your feeling is not acceptable or not allowed or not a big deal or anything else that keeps you removed from it, you follow up with *and I am still sad that I did not get a chance to do [x]*. Most likely your brain will then try to find a new reason why you are not allowed to feel the feeling, and again you bring yourself back to the feeling.

I needed a script when I first started this practice because it felt so far from where my mind was trying to take me. It turned out the script I needed was very simple: *I am feeling [feeling] because [thing that happened] and it is okay to feel that.*

It is deceptively simple. In fact, it feels so simple and childish that it could not possibly have any power. But it works and here is how.

To go back to the previous example, you feel the early tinge of sadness when you watch a teen movie and see a bunch of happy kids going to prom. You realize you wish you could have worn the clothes you wanted to wear and gone with a person of a different gender than the person you actually did go with. Your mind starts sprinting to shut it down.

You should be grateful. Your mom spent a lot of money to rent you that outfit. There are a bunch of people who do not even get to go to prom. What a first-world problem. Prom was 15 years ago!

But then you breathe and give yourself permission to feel the emotion.

I am feeling sad because I did not get to be comfortable and open at prom and it is okay to feel that.

Hmm debatable; is it really okay? You stop, you breathe again, you return to the feeling.

Yes, I feel sad because prom was not fun or safe the way it was for other people and it is okay to feel that.

You are a grown-ass adult, are you really going to be sad about prom? Prom?! You need to get your shit together and stop whining.

> *I am allowed to feel sad. I am sad because prom was not the joyful experience it was for my friends and it is okay to feel that.*

You get the picture. The ability to feel the feeling is an underworked muscle. It is so hard to hold on to because you have not practiced holding it. In fact, you were probably practicing the exact opposite. By continually and gently bringing yourself back to the feeling, you build this muscle and it becomes stronger. This practice takes you away from the story of what the feeling should be and returns you to what it is. This can also be done by stepping out of the thoughts and into the physical sensations. Your brain is trying to do the work of solving the problem or evading the pain, while your body simply needs to experience the sensations.

With practice, you go from being able to hold on to it from one second to two seconds, from two seconds to five seconds, from five seconds to ten seconds. Feeling the feeling eventually does not feel so impossible or threatening. It could certainly stay uncomfortable, but that is okay too. Sadness and anger and jealousy and these other pieces of grief can be considered "negative emotions" because no one is having a good time while they experience them. People avoid them because they feel so unpleasant, and anything you are trying to avoid is negative, right? A more useful framing is calling them uncomfortable emotions. It makes sense to try to avoid a "negative emotion," but by framing the emotion as simply uncomfortable, you can accept first that you are able to live through discomfort and second that there can still be benefits to uncomfortable things.

What exactly is the benefit of feeling a feeling and not trying to avoid it? You can finally put it down. If you gently allow yourself to feel a feeling without judgment or shame or a desire to experience something different than what you are actually feeling, then you can move through it and leave it behind. You can integrate the experience into your memories and your life and you can feel less hijacked by the unprocessed feelings. And then you can see what is on the other side of them. Ironically, by trying to avoid feelings, you simply end up experiencing them longer.

A note on anger

When it comes to the uncomfortable emotions, anger can get the worst rep. Not only can it feel useless, but it can feel dangerous too. If you have spent any part of your life around a person who became violent when they got angry, you might fear losing control in that same way. It feels crucial to never express the anger because you assume if the anger becomes too big, you could be just as violent or abusive as that person. Fortunately, anger does not work that way. There is no threshold of anger where it becomes so big that it suddenly becomes violence. For people who do become violent or abusive when they are angry, it is generally because they have had that kind of behavior modeled for them in the past, and they do not have other coping mechanisms to manage it.[24]

Simply feeling anger on its own is not destructive. It is not inherently bad or evil or a sin. It is a feeling that provides information, just like any other feeling. Anger is not destructive until it leads to destructive action. While that sounds obvious, the shame that can come along with anger can lead you to believe that the feeling itself is the problem. It is not.

Anger is a protector. It can stand as protection over fear and sadness, which feel more raw and vulnerable. This is why anger is sometimes labeled a secondary emotion. When it comes to trans grief, anger is certainly a protector. Anger shouts that the way you were forced to grow up and the ways you were forced to hide yourself were not fair. And they weren't. Stepping into that anger of "it's not fair" can feel safer than exposing the vulnerable sadness of "and I didn't deserve it."

The goal is not to reject any of these feelings but to accept the ways they have served you. "It's not fair *and* I didn't deserve it."

Anger and sadness both serve purposes and provide pieces of the message. Instead of feeling shame around experiencing anger, you can thank it for the ways it has protected you. Allow your anger to be purposeful (rather than meaningless) and then appreciate its purpose. Anger wanted you to live a life with justice and safety and with your needs fulfilled. The life of a trans person lacks those at foundational points. Your anger wanted better for you and knew you deserved better. Your anger was an act of your body's love. By acknowledging it and accepting it, you allow it to move through you and not set up permanent camp inside your body.

CHAPTER 12

Depression and Anxiety Become Habits

Another barrier in transition is that sometimes the circumstances of your life legitimately feel as if they are improving compared with past struggles but it seems as if your mental health has not caught up. The long-term mental health effects of living with dysphoria or distress can take on many forms. Anxiety/social anxiety, depression, dissociation, and other trauma responses are common and sometimes long lasting, and your brain gets good at things it does consistently. This is usually a good thing. It would be terrible to have to focus as hard on tying your shoes as you did when you first learned how as a child. Instead, you got better and better at it and your brain created a neurological pathway that was well trodden. The more your brain goes down a pathway, the faster it is to travel down it. Now you are an adult and you can tie your shoes quickly and on autopilot. Even far more complex tasks like driving a car become second nature and you feel comfortable changing lanes on the highway while talking to your friend in the passenger seat and simultaneously changing the radio station. After a certain amount of time your brain says, *Oh, I've got this, I know how this goes, I can do it without conscious effort*. It allows those actions to be performed without conscious thought so that you can focus on other tasks. However, this is not always convenient when it comes to something like depression.

Depression

When your brain becomes good at depression, it also tries to save you time. In the past, if someone misgendered you in a store, it might have triggered a series of thoughts like, *What happened? Was it the way I was walking? Is it my height? Is it my voice?*

That becomes, *I don't know why I even bother. No one is ever going to see me as my gender*, which turns into, *Life is always going to be like this. Can I survive another 50 years of this feeling?*

Which becomes, *Absolutely not, I can barely tolerate it now*, which then becomes, *This feeling has to stop somehow and if I can't make people stop misgendering me, maybe I should just end things now.*

You ride that mental pathway enough times and your brain says, *Oh, I see where we're going. I can get us there faster!* Then someone misgenders you in the store on a different occasion and your brain jumps over all the middle thoughts and takes you straight to *maybe I should just end things* in about a millisecond. This is very hard to argue with. It happens so fast and you definitively interpret it as truth.

Treatment for depression can involve a lot of different kinds of interventions, and one can be slowing down that thought process, being able to identify the middle thoughts and challenging them. It is a lot easier to challenge *no one is ever going to see me as my gender* than it is to challenge the thought that chants *time to die*. This is not to say any of that process is easy, but it gives you a lot more ammunition to fight against the extremely nihilistic voice.

Yet even if you are not engaged in some therapeutic process of challenging those internal voices, physical transition can affect the frequency with which you get misgendered. Which is to say, your internal dialogue might be exactly what it has always been, but the way people are responding to you is different. Maybe you are getting misgendered in stores less and less, but when it does happen your brain still picks up that nihilistic script. This can be confusing. What do you do when your life is improving and your brain is still telling you everything is hopeless and nothing will ever get better and you should die?

First, you respond by being kind to yourself. If you have suicidal thoughts, then you have spent years needing those suicidal thoughts. This might sound counterintuitive, but it is true. People have suicidal thoughts because they are comforting. If you have absolutely no control over the way people treat you and the chaos around you, then frequently the most comforting thought you could have is, *If it gets too bad, I can still escape.* Yes, sometimes that means escaping life. Even the fantasy of running away to a new city, state, or even country is not sufficient if you are certain you will still be mistreated in any new location. Then suicide becomes the ultimate protective measure against an intolerable life. You needed that assurance at some point in your life.

The least you could do for yourself is to think of that younger version of yourself who was hurting and gently and kindly understand what they were going through. Gently understand why suicide was such a necessary possibility to hold. And gently return to your present self and acknowledge that you needed that for a long time and your brain is really used to going there when things get scary or hard.

A lot of times people think recovery means that they will never be depressed again or never have those suicidal thoughts again. I do not necessarily think that is the case. What I think happens for many people is that the depressive episodes become shorter, more manageable, and less overwhelming. Suicide does not feel like it is at the top of the list and it gets pushed down by healthier coping mechanisms. Chances are, when you were in your darkest place, someone would suggest some common coping mechanism like journaling or meditation or going for a walk, and you would laugh and think how this person has clearly misunderstood how dark things are in your brain and how none of that would do anything for you. But as your life improves, you may find that journaling or meditation or going for a walk feel nice. Maybe your list of coping mechanisms has those at the top, or maybe it has things like playing video games, or cooking, or talking to friends, or punching a punching bag, or masturbating. And as you fill your list, suicidal thoughts get pushed down to 10th on the list, then 100th on the list, and then 3000th on the list. A situation in which the first 2999 things on the list did not help you feel better would certainly be dire, but it is possible. Keeping this "out" on your list (albeit really, really far down on the list) does not mean you are broken. It means you still need an option for an emergency backup plan in case things really go to shit. Someone telling you that you are never allowed to think about suicide ever again, first, is not realistic, but actually it would be terrifying for a lot of people. It is comforting because it is an out, and the way to stop thinking about it is by living a life that does not feel like it needs an out, not by having it ripped out of your hands as an option, and not by getting really good at white-knuckling it through pain and tragedy.

Anxiety

Anxiety can also be a very common feeling for trans people and a hard one to shake. Like depression, it also becomes a habit after years of practice, and like depression, anxiety is also doing its best to protect us. Fears and anxieties become very loud because we figure if we focus on future problems, then we can prevent them. Your mind anticipates a possible problem, and it starts doing everything it can to try to make sure that the harm is mitigated as much as possible. Anxiety's ideal scenario is to avoid the iceberg entirely, but if the ship is going to hit it, then maybe there is a way to get everyone on a lifeboat. You think about one scenario, then ten scenarios, then one hundred scenarios, then one thousand scenarios. You figure if you can anticipate exactly what will occur, then you will be prepared and you will be as unharmed as you can possibly be. Except it never actually works out that way. What happens is that the longer you are given to imagine scenarios, the more you will find other possibilities. You could be pushing a million scenarios and still be far from imagining every possible outcome. And then when the event finally occurs, it is never exactly how you imagined it. Which means first that all the prep work was of questionable use, and second that you had to live maybe a hundred or a thousand or a million distressing scenarios in your own mind.

If a scenario is going to be distressing, then you might as well only experience that distress once. No matter what happens, you will have to figure out how to respond as it unfolds. There is no way to rehearse and practice something that you do not even know the details of yet. Even if you have your script for the role you will play, other people are not going to read their lines the way you wrote them. They do not know what you wrote for them. You only have control of your part, and everyone else's will be a mystery until it happens.

Allow yourself to experience something 0–1 times, rather than 2–2,000,000 times in imagined anticipation. I realize that this is easier said than done, and your brain will continue to try to do what it is used to and problem solve the future unknown issues. When that happens, you will also gently bring yourself back to the present, the way you have with other uncomfortable feelings.

If you have ever done any meditation or mindfulness exercises, this may feel familiar. I like to imagine that there is a part of my mind that is a small toddler who I am babysitting. This child keeps trying to get into dangerous parts of the house and my job as a babysitter is to make sure that no one gets hurt. Maybe the child keeps trying to touch the hot stovetop while food is cooking, and I have to keep going over to the stove and picking up the child and saying, *Hey how about we come over here and draw?* And then maybe the child goes back over to the stove and again I go over to them and pick them up and say, *Hey, do you want to watch a movie? Or play with your stuffed animals?* No matter how many times they try to touch the hot stove, I gently redirect them. And the gentle part is very important, because while it may be tempting to yell at this toddler, they will most likely just be upset and not learn what you want them to learn because they are too busy being terrified by the yelling. The gentleness and consistency are key.

Your brain keeps trying to jump into a fantasy scenario that you think you are using to prepare yourself for the future, when actually are just activating yourself with it. When that happens, then you gently redirect yourself back to the present. Redirecting yourself can look like anything, but it takes some gentle acknowledgment that what you are doing is not the most useful or soothing thing to do and that you are not at the scary event yet. For me sometimes it looks like repeating, *I know you're stressed out about that, but it hasn't happened yet and you won't know how to respond until you get there, so for right now you are safe and fine and okay.* It can be similar to the kind of script around sadness or anger. Guided meditations will often tell you to return your thoughts to your breath or your body. Similarly, this is just a mindful way to acknowledge the feeling and bring yourself back to the present.

You repeat your redirection as often as you need to, and the more you repeat it, the easier it gets and the quicker you notice when you are slipping into those anticipatory fantasies. The muscle of returning to the present becomes stronger. And with the gentleness, you prevent yourself from adding a level of shame to your anxiety. (Any feeling added to the shame of feeling an emotion just gives you more layers to extricate yourself from. Allow yourself to simply have feelings on their own, rather than feelings and feelings about your feelings.) You can stay in the present where you have only the problems of the present and not the potential problems of the future too.

CHAPTER 13

Being Trans in a Transphobic Society Can Be Traumatic

When people think of trauma they often think of large, singular events like being mugged or attacked, being in a car crash, or surviving a natural disaster. There are few long-term events that are included in the cultural definition of trauma, but the ones that are tend to be around enormous experiences like living through war or violent political upheaval. There are many long-term events that do not often get included when people discuss trauma. Even experiences as unfortunately common as child abuse can get lost among others that seem more dramatic or obvious. When you begin to include the complex stories of long-term trauma, it can also make it more difficult to understand how the harm was enacted and how the survivor was affected. A singular traumatic event has a clear beginning and end, but when it comes to long-term experiences of trauma, we are left to wonder what happens when you are unable to escape the experience. What does it mean to live in an ongoing experience of trauma? How does it affect the survivor long term?

If you get into a car crash, it may take a very long time to feel comfortable getting in a car again, but being in other spaces like your home might feel okay. On the other hand, standing next to a road might feel much less okay. There are likely places that feel less dangerous than others. But what happens when the whole world feels unsafe? These issues can add a level of complexity not only to understanding the experiences themselves but also to understanding the ways in which our bodies and minds process the trauma.

If you are trans, then there are times when the world feels unsafe. Transphobia is not a singular, identifiable threat. The potential for it exists all around. Even when you are around people who are not actively or intentionally transphobic, transphobia can seep into the foundations of our daily lives. In a society where being cisgender is the norm, and everyone is cisgender until proven otherwise, then transgender people become outsiders, or the other. Sometimes being the other just means being different or in a statistically small category, but usually there are more implications to being othered. It can mean the world sees you as an oddity, or a freak, or a person with a mental illness. It might mean when you are desired, you are objectified or fetishized. It is not an enjoyable experience, and it is increasingly detrimental to a person's mental health the longer it continues. It is impossible to not internalize that transphobia to some degree.

Many trans people have to work through their learned disgust around trans people before they can acknowledge they might be trans themselves. It is also generally hard to identify those feelings as internalized transphobia. They can be as subtle as *I just don't think I'm like those people*. It can take time to realize that the reason you don't feel like those people is because you have made some assumption about those people's lives and you think all trans people are sad, or maybe even delusional. You think they do not have authentic loving relationships or that they don't have careers or families. You have attached a judgment to the assumptions and have decided you do not want to be included within that category. Not to mention the blending of other internalized biases (like racism, sexism, ableism, sizeism, stigma against sex work, and so on). This is all learned from the way we hear people talk about trans people and the way the media talks about trans people. Our first mental images of trans people usually come secondhand from these narratives rather than from knowing a trans person personally. We do not hear from trans people before we hear about trans people, and we learn disgust before all else. This undoubtedly affects our thoughts about ourselves and our own genders. This also has the potential to be traumatic.

If the first time you watch a movie with a trans character and you start to think, *Oh, I might have something in common with this character*, and your dad, sitting on the couch next to you, laughs and makes a derogatory comment, whatever happened in that moment of identification will be squashed. You will learn that you cannot be like that person even if you do not fully understand what that person is and why you identify with them. You have already learned to start shutting yourself down. Of course, you do this as a matter of safety; you don't want to be taunted or harassed or attacked or disowned. But each time you shut yourself down you start to split off from yourself. You start compartmentalizing different aspects of who you are and where it is safe to share and express those aspects. Trauma can begin a process of fragmentation of your identity, where parts of yourself must be kept separate from other parts of yourself so that you can be safe and survive your environment. Depending on your home or school life, those safe spaces may feel miniscule or nonexistent. You begin acting. You begin pretending to be the person who other people want and expect you to be. This can also be traumatic.

Eventually you might have been doing this for so long that you forget that you are doing it. You forget that moment of identification when you were watching that movie with your dad when you were seven years old. You forget that time in kindergarten when they split the class into boys and girls and someone told you that you were in the wrong line. You forget those feelings in the pit of your stomach when someone told you how pretty you looked in a dress or how handsome you looked in a suit at your cousin's wedding.

It is easier to push all of that away than it is to feel it. Instead we push all of that into a deep, dark closet in our brain and lock it up. This is why lots of people don't come out until adulthood. All of those feelings were locked away and forgotten about as a matter of safety.

Trauma can also affect memory in significant ways. Traumatic events can lead to memories either being remembered in extreme detail or barely remembered at all. When stress hormones flood the brain during a traumatic event, it can mean that the early parts of the event are remembered in extreme detail and, as the stress hormones continue to flood the brain, the brain's ability to encode the memory becomes impaired. Often people who have experienced traumatic events have some memories that they feel are "burned into" their brain and others feel like a blur or that it is impossible to pin down details.

In my own life, I assumed for many years that I had a terrible memory and I struggled to remember many parts of my life pre-transition. I would read through old posts I had written online and old journal entries and feel like they were written by another person. It was a person who felt vaguely familiar, but I certainly did not feel as if I was personally connected to them. I could not remember having written those words or having thought those thoughts. It wasn't until I looked back at entries I had written in 2012 compared with things I had written in 2013 (when I began my physical transition) that I noticed there was a drastic and sudden stark difference in my memory. I could not remember any of my writing from 2012, or even being that 2012 person, and then everything from 2013 onward felt a part of the history of my life. I recognized it as me! This reflection was the first time I had considered that my memory could have been affected by the difficulty of my pre-transition life. The evidence was hard to refute. What other reason would there be that I was not able to place anything that happened in December 2012 and could suddenly access everything from January 2013 and on? There was no other sudden change aside from the fact that, perhaps for the first time in my life, I had a sense of self to attach my memories to. To me, that felt like the difference: All my life I had had experiences but nothing to pin them to. Almost as if I had been trying to file away information without a filing cabinet or a hard drive. The memories had nowhere to land. Of course, I had memories of my past, but they were inconsistent and fuzzy. In order to keep memories as a story of my self, it turns out I needed a sense of self.

There is currently little to no research around that kind of traumatic memory loss for trans people, but it is safe to assume the trauma of growing up as a trans person would function in a similar way to other forms of long-term trauma. Many trans people note some level of memory loss or difficulty accessing past chunks of their lives. If nothing else, it seemed that my own mind said, *Are you sure we need to hold on to those memories? We were having a really bad time and perhaps those experiences don't need to go in the scrapbook.*

As we know, not everyone who experiences an extreme event is always traumatized by it. Some soldiers return from war and are diagnosed with post-traumatic stress disorder, and some are not. That is because whether we experience something as trauma or not has a lot to do with whether we are capable of coping with the event that is occurring. Some trauma experts have called trauma an experience that overwhelms our ability to cope.[25]

This means that someone who is trained for and is expecting a certain high-intensity event may not experience the event as traumatic. For example, a self-defense instructor may have the ability to react to being mugged far differently than someone who does not have that skillset or training. After hours of practice, they can respond quickly and easily to a physical attack in a way that many people could not. Instead of responding with a flight or flee response, they can fight back competently and without feeling overwhelmed by the scenario. They know exactly how they will respond because that response is practiced and habitual. For most of us, our responses in those high-intensity experiences are just as much a surprise to us as anyone else.

But because trauma is an experience that is dependent on whether we have the ability to cope with a stressor, this also means that potentially traumatic events experienced in childhood are more likely to lead to trauma responses than those experienced in adulthood. Research shows that diagnoses like PTSD, agoraphobia, and panic disorder are more likely in children who experienced a potentially traumatic event than adults who experience the same. Children are extremely limited in coping mechanisms, and children are also far more likely to experience feelings of helplessness and a lack of control. It is unlikely a child is going to feel prepared for many stressors at all. They simply do not have the skills or practice that could allow those experiences to feel manageable.

Of course, it is not a personal failing to be unable to cope with a potentially traumatic experience, and regardless of whether overwhelming events are experienced in childhood or adulthood, they are never the fault of the person experiencing them. But this also may point to one reason why trans people are more likely to experience trauma responses—this kind of overwhelming experience can begin extremely early in life. Trans people are exposed to transphobia often before they are even aware that they are trans themselves. The violent messages become internalized before there is time for that kind of self-discovery. And when your initial messages about trans people are filled with disgust and disdain, then it becomes all the more difficult to accept that it might be an identity that you hold.

The higher levels of discrimination and oppression faced by trans people would be enough to explain those higher rates of trauma, but I suspect the young age at which trans people begin to hear and internalize transphobic messages compounds the risk.

The inner child

The concept of the inner child is one most people have heard at some point and may have positive or negative associations with.

At this point it has been incorporated into a lot of practices and theories, but for some it is an idea that feels like a goofy framing by New Age hippies and psychologists in silk scarves. The original concept of the inner child simply states that we all carry around a younger version of ourselves, and the concept likely goes back to Carl Jung's child archetype, which has evolved over time with different theorists. That internal younger self may still experience the world the way a child does. This can look like having tantrums when things do not go our way, and it can look like a need to create and play. The inner child is not meant to be a solely positive or negative archetype, simply one who longs for a kind of simplicity or innocence in a different way than adulthood requires.

Regardless of if specific inner child theories personally resonate with you, it is true that many trans people experience a need to re-examine their childhood and adolescence, and some do feel a need to specifically reconnect with those younger parts of themselves. Childhood and adolescence can both be times that trans people feel they have a lot of unfinished business from. There is the unfinished business of grief that we have discussed, but there can also be stages of development that may feel unfulfilled and ones that feel interrupted by trauma.

If there is anything that the field of psychology has, it is an abundance of theories of development. Attachment theory, the hierarchy of needs, and newer theories like the emotional security theory all see childhood safety and security as a primary goal of early stages of development. Safety, of course, does not just mean safety from physical harm. Growing up with an experience of gender that does not fit in to society's or your family's expectations can feel emotionally treacherous and unsafe.

Perhaps then when you look at the facts that the development of a trans child is potentially traumatic (for all the reasons listed above) and that many trans adults find the need to reconnect with their inner child, it makes sense that the practice of reconnecting with our inner child might be one that attempts to create a sense of safety that was not there initially.

Unfortunately, the unfinished work of creating safety for yourself is not something that ever goes away if you ignore it. For a trans person who spent years of life just keeping their head above water, finally beginning to have an authentic experience of their gender is often the first time they start experiencing feelings as they are rather than running from them. This can feel like being thrown into the deep end of all your psychological shit. This can be specific to gender, but it can also bring up countless issues around your upbringing and family and relational dynamics and other issues all at once and all together.

While dissociation[26] and compartmentalization[27] are extremely normal ways of surviving something that feels too big and inescapable, they are not permanent solutions. The act of transitioning or being intentional about your gender is entirely the opposite experience of dissociation and compartmentalization. And dropping those methods of getting through life can sometimes feel like dropping a kind of armor or protective barrier. Living life without those levels of dissociation can feel like walking around like an exposed nerve—everything is too bright and harsh and abrasive. This is a completely normal experience, and it is also a completely unpleasant experience.

Inner child work (or if that phrase is not your favorite, reconnecting with a younger version of yourself) can look like a number of different things that heal those early wounds and create that sense of safety in the present. For some this feels like a spiritual experience and for others it can feel more practical. But it hinges on determining what kind of adult you needed as a child and being that for yourself now.

As absurd as it can feel, I suggest writing on paper or speaking to your younger self out loud. For the same reasons that this was helpful while dealing with anger, it allows your mind to slow down and not jump to the old patterns of thought. Also, by doing this you can create the kind of separation you need to be able to see your adult self and your child self as separate parts of your whole self. You can see the child part of you that is scared and in need of reassurance and you can see the adult who has more agency and skills that can help that child. You get to play both roles and make space for each role to speak and be heard.

When you start to keep an eye out for your inner child, they get easier to notice. The times when you feel like having a tantrum, or pouting, or start feeling small and wanting to shrink into a corner are often times when that little kid wants to be noticed. And those can be the best times to check in with them. You can start by asking what they need and listening to the answer. The goal is to not shut down any of the answers with adult logic or shame but instead to hear what they need and see if you, as a caring adult, can provide it. Maybe they need reassurance, maybe they need privacy, maybe they need to feel protected and defended, maybe they need rest or play. Tell them that you understand how they feel and you will make sure to get them what they need. Tell them that they are doing great and you love them very much. Be the adult that the child needed and still needs.

Try holding your arms or putting your hand on your chest as you say it. And if you feel comfortable doing so, speak to that child part of you out loud. The physical actions of touch and verbal speech allow you to escape the old mental scripts. You escape all the skillful intellectualization that so deftly avoids the feelings. By doing this, you can hold the part of you that needs reassurance. I promise you will feel completely ridiculous the first time you try, and I promise that it is worth trying anyway. The more you do this, the more you will feel integrated with that part of yourself, and that little kid will begin to heal.

The inner adolescent

The concept of the inner adolescent is much less discussed but is exactly what you think it is: your teenage self in all of their awkward, rebellious, unruly, confused, stressed out glory carried within you.

Erik Erikson's theory of psychosocial development, one of the most prominent theories of development, considers adolescence a time of either identity formation or role confusion. According to this theory, it is a time when a teenager either establishes a strong sense of self and feeling of control over their life (identity formation) or they do not (role confusion). The way to successfully complete this phase of development is to have the space and ability to try on different identities and keep what works and shed what does not. While for some that might be a goth phase, for others it may be the ability to truly try on their gender, and for plenty of people it is both. If inner child work is about reconnecting with safety, then the work of reconnecting with your inner adolescent is about working out and integrating your identity.

Adolescents have a need to integrate their various identities and determine what aspects of themselves are important to their sense of self. They also have a strong need to feel acknowledged and understood. This is not always an opportunity that is afforded to trans people. As we discussed, trans people sometimes instead have to deal with the identity fragmentation caused by discrimination and transphobia. This fragmentation or the afore-mentioned role confusion results in more unfinished business. The question of gender identity in adulthood can thrust someone back into that unresolved work of the first adolescence.[28]

Many trans people felt as if their first adolescence was a process of going through the motions, or even of trying to mimic the behaviors of the other teenagers around them. External markers of adolescence, like dating and fashion, felt complicated, but so did these much deeper concepts that adolescents grapple with like, *What kind of person am I and what kind of person do I want to become?*

In order to answer these questions, you must examine the values and stories that were handed to you by your family and determine if those are ones that you plan to hold on to or aban-don. Determining whether you are going to continue to stay in line with your family's values, religion, or politics is a huge piece of the work of adolescence. Not only that, but it can also be a time to determine how you integrate aspects of your narrative. For example, do you think about your ethnicity or culture the same way your parents do? Do you have a new experience of your culture due to being raised in a different setting than your parents? Does being first or second or third generation mean your experience of your culture is different than your parents'? Are your parents different races or ethnicities from one another, and how do you combine those aspects of yourself? Or maybe you are a different race than the people who raised you, and if so, how do understand and integrate all of it? Do you plan to continue traditional cultural practices or modernize? You finally reach an age where you can begin to do and see things differently than your caregivers, and that can come with a lot of existential questions like, *Who am I and what am I doing here?*

Certainly gender is going to be a large part of those questions if you are anything other than strictly cisgender. Even if you were completely unaware of your trans identity as a teenager, there will have been aspects of other people's adolescent process that felt entirely foreign. While it can feel possible to "get away with" not completely meeting gendered expectations as a small child, those expectations are enforced more severely as puberty hits. These expectations are enforced by adults who see this as a time when you need to learn how to properly be a man or woman, and they are enforced by other adolescents who are attempting to seem in the know. The flexibility that might have been afforded to a gender nonconforming child and their gender expression is revoked, and rules and standards take its place. Attempting to meet these standards when they feel like they are being spoken in a foreign language can be anything from awkward to traumatic.

Cis people might not notice the arbitrariness of a message like, *Half of all people must shave their legs and armpits while the other half are strictly prohibited from doing so*, but when the standard used against you is not in alignment with your sense of self, then it is almost impossible *not* to notice.

Yet adolescents also are working hard to understand their relationships and connections for the first time, and there is a strong need to fit in. Adolescents are learning and fine-tuning social skills around developing more intimate relationships than they had in childhood. These are crucial skills to have, but there can be the downsides of seeming too preoccupied with peer approval. Whether teens are actually too preoccupied or not is debatable, but the fact is that sometimes the desire to fit in and the desire to figure out your own personal needs can clash. The desire to fit in and not be shunned by your peers usually wins out over trying to be someone far outside the gender norms.

This can result in the splitting off or fragmentation that we mentioned. And sometimes you role-play or act for such a long time that you forget that you are doing it, and it takes well into the process of transition to notice where things still feel disconnected.

Inner adolescent work can be reconnecting to what you split off from and putting all the pieces back together. There are many ways this can be done, and the practicalities of accessing your inner moody teen might not be any different than accessing your inner child. The content, on the other hand, will be entirely different. The insecurities from the first time around will come up. These can be the kinds of questions that might feel too silly or vain to take seriously as an adult: *Am I cool enough? Am I interesting enough? Am I hot enough?*

It could look like tapping into a personal sense of self that does want to see what it is like to dye your hair blue or get a nose piercing. These could feel frivolous, but there is likely some element of them that are a means to getting to what you did not have the chance to process and integrate the first time around.

See what happens when you give those questions space before shutting them down. There is a great deal to be found in the answers, but more importantly there is the healing experience of respecting your adolescent needs.

The experience of returning to earlier developmental stages as an adult can be unnerving. It returns you to the challenges of development, but it can also return you to the more specific challenges that you were experiencing at those ages. In other words, a feeling of a second adolescence can bring up feelings around puberty and adolescence, but it can also bring up the pain of your parents' divorce if that occurred during first adolescence. It can bring up the feelings of food insecurity or abuse or abandonment or displacement if those were things you experienced in your first adolescence. We find long-forgotten feelings while traversing similar pathways. It is hard to feel prepared for those startling landmarks on the path, and there is likely no way to prepare for them in advance. It is important to know that that is normal and to do the work to surround yourself with the resources you initially needed as an adolescent and did not have access to. Now can be a chance to have the healthiest experience of your childhood or adolescence.

CHAPTER 14

The Common Intersection Between Trans and Neurodivergent Identities

Different forms of neurodivergence can frequently appear hand in hand with trans identities. No one knows exactly why this is, but it is fair to say that autism spectrum disorder (ASD) and attention deficit hyperactivity disorder (ADHD) are very common among trans people. The most current research has shown that individuals in the trans community are three to six times more likely than cis people to be autistic. The same study shows that trans individuals score higher on measures of autistic traits, that trans people have higher rates of other neurodevelopmental and psychiatric conditions, and that trans people are more likely to suspect that they have undiagnosed autism than cis people.[29] Other studies have similarly confirmed higher rates of ASD and ADHD in their samples.

There is a lot to be said about neurodivergence under a medical model. Many people are challenging a model that sees neurodivergence as a disorder—rather than simply alternate neurotypes[30]—compared with something called "neurotypical." Similar to transgender identity, you can certainly challenge the whole system that places some common identities as privileged and correct identities.[31]

For trans people at this intersection of identities, there is a compounded stigmatization and invalidation that complicates the process of identifying their gender identity. As common as this intersection of identities is, they are two stigmatized identities that combined can receive a mess of prejudice and discrimination.

Ironically in this case, neurodivergence gets diagnosed at different rates based on gender. Much like the rest of medicine, the standards were set by and according to the presentation of cisgender males. Anyone whose experience exists outside of that model goes unnoticed. Not only do cisgender women struggle to learn about their neurotype, but trans people break open the mold of what is considered the girl vs. boy/woman vs. man presentations. With higher rates of neurodivergence in the trans community, but also lower rates of identifying neurodivergence outside of the cis male framework, there is a lot that goes unnoticed and misunderstood.

Infantilization[32] is common and contributes to the invalidation of the experiences of trans neurodivergent people. Media portrayals of neurodivergent people are almost exclusively of children, and resources for ASD and ADHD are frequently in connection to schools and therefore accessible only to children and adolescents. Even clinicians are frequently taught about working with these neurotypes as if they disappear in adulthood. Of course, neurodivergent adults don't cease to exist, but you might think that, seeing how little space they are given in the conversation.

This becomes the first layer of systemic infantilization—where many people can only imagine neurodivergent children and adolescents because those are the only images that have been presented. Countless articles have been written about neurodivergent youth (often in the case of parenting or school settings), but when you look for that same kind of information about adults, the numbers drop suddenly and starkly. The second layer of infantilization occurs when neurodivergent adults are seen as childlike or not matured to the same degree as neurotypical adults. They are deemed incapable of making choices for themselves even in adulthood. And instead of blaming the real barriers, such as the lack of accommodations and understanding, it is seen as a personal failing that neurodivergent adults may struggle in jobs or higher education. Doctors, therapists, teachers, and family members all play a part in this process.

When this intersects with gender identity, it can lead to narratives like the untrue belief that neurodivergent people are less able to know or incapable of knowing whether they are trans or not. And that creates an even more reinforced barrier than already exists within transphobia alone. Sometimes this looks like a parent's concern that their child's attention on their gender is merely "another hyperfixation."[33] Sometimes this looks like therapists extending the number of sessions necessary for a neurodivergent client to receive the authorization for medical care, perhaps believing that this client does not understand what is at stake, or that they are mistaking some other experience for feelings of gender dysphoria. These are extremely harmful messages and contribute to confusion, doubt, and frustration. Because most people encounter gatekeepers who are both cisgender and neurotypical, this means dealing with barriers of not only subtle or not-so-subtle transphobia but also ableism.

Even the most confident person will struggle to navigate a field of clinical landmines like this one.

Neurodiverse trans people I have spoken to mention additional questions they had to grapple with (in addition to all the other ones mentioned in this book) in order to determine their gender identity. One is a feeling of being alienated by gender and the ways in which people describe it. For some, gender was never something they expected to feel right or natural. If the way that gender is described feels removed from your experience in the first place, then it is not surprising that it can feel extremely difficult to know if the narratives around gender feel alienating in the "regular" neurodivergent way or the trans neurodivergent way.

Some neurodivergent people express feeling dissociated from their emotions in a way that made it particularly difficult to notice uncomfortable feelings around gender. It can take an initial process of figuring out how to identify and process experiences that are described by neurotypical people in extremely different ways. If dysphoria, or even just emotions generally, is always described through a language that feels unrelatable or inaccessible, then there will be a barrier to receiving internal messages. It can take time to notice that you are dissociating before you can even begin to ask what you are dissociating from. Then the response to that question may not be a simple and straightforward single answer.

Masking[34] neurodivergent traits in order to be seen and respected by neurotypical people is often an exhausting demand. Ableism and transphobia create very credible threats to enforce compliance. Which means for some, it becomes difficult to stop masking, even in cases where it is not being demanded of them and it is safe (or safer) to drop. But masking, coupled with a pressure to appear cis, can create a feeling that not only is this necessary but surely there must be some reward for putting on the show. It is hard to feel that so much of your defense mechanisms moving through the world might just be because the world can be cruel. And when those defenses (like masking and attempting to be cis) are something that you have done for a long time, it can be easier to believe that this is something that is worth doing rather than something that is being externally and intrusively enforced. There can be a lot of processing in the realization that you were kept from ways of living that would allow you to thrive. There are so many layers of pulling that apart that unlearning the internalized ableism and unlearning the internalized transphobia can take years. It can feel like it can be too hard to categorize certain life experiences as a "trans thing" or a "neurodivergent thing." And in fact, many don't find it possible to.

The term "autigender"[55] was created by those who don't feel it is possible to separate their autistic identity from their trans identity and the two are so intertwined that it would be absurd to try. Both are extremely foundational identity experiences so this is not surprising, and of course it is one of the very many ways to experience gender. Unfortunately, this is not always what doctors or clinicians want to hear. The gatekeeper model is obsessed with diagnosis and obsessed with categorization. A label like autigender challenges that system entirely. The gatekeeper model believes in a fantasy of a pure unadulterated trans experience and a pure unadulterated neurodivergent experience. But humans are not so simple. People with both experiences describe being young and not knowing if people in their lives were reacting to certain actions and presentations that didn't fit into a gender box or that didn't fit into a social interaction box. For example, did you cut all your hair off for gender reasons or because you were "just a weird kid"? And if people believed you were a "weird kid," did it really matter? The dismissive assessment doesn't bother pulling the pieces apart; it is hypocritical that it would be held against you as an adult for not pulling the pieces apart either. The label autigender says all of those experiences are interconnected and there is no need to categorize them for the comfort of allistic[36] cis people. This term is one way that neurodivergent trans people have reclaimed an experience that has historically been gatekept and not been allowed to be self-defined.

Finally, executive dysfunction[37] is also a very common experience for neurodivergent people. This can be extremely frustrating on its own but can become overwhelming for someone who is trying to seek trans-related care in a gatekeeper model. The gatekeeper model is one that demands jumping through hoop after hoop according to the standards of the gatekeeper. This is anything from paperwork to appointments to phone calls to navigating insurance. The system was not built to be simple to navigate and is in fact intended to be actively discouraging.

Informed consent care is increasing accessibility but remains far from perfect. Advocating for yourself can become exhausting and it is important to allow yourself rest. Also allow yourself the knowledge that the system is failing you. When at all possible, find people who can advocate for you on your behalf. That can be as simple as asking someone to make a phone call for you, make an appointment for you, or do preliminary research for you in order to send you a manageable amount of resources to look through. It can feel hard to ask for help, even from people who are being paid to help (like therapists, nurses, or front desk staff), but when a system is doing everything it can to discourage you, then you have no need to feel shame or guilt about getting whatever benefits you can manage.

CHAPTER 15

Seeking More Help

The previous chapters are of course not a complete list of mental health issues that can be experienced alongside gender dysphoria. They simply cover some of the more common experiences and how to begin to consider and possibly address how they interconnect with your gender identity. You might find that addressing your trans identity could ease many other distressing symptoms, but some pieces may still be left over. Or, of course, you may find that you ease a lot of your gender-related distress, and you still have anxiety, depression, trauma, executive dysfunction, or many other issues that have nothing to do with gender and never did. You may need a lot more help than this book can offer, and that is more than okay. That is not a sign of weakness. Being trans can be exhausting, and at times it can exacerbate what already felt difficult to manage.

Disordered eating and substance abuse frequently exist alongside gender dysphoria and they are not discussed specifically here. Trans people have many coping mechanisms for dealing with the distress and discomfort of gender dysphoria and all of those coping mechanisms may need tailored interventions.

Trauma, for instance, can have long-lasting effects on the

body that may need specialized and personalized care. Commonly discussed techniques like mindfulness can sometimes make traumatized individuals feel more activated than before. This is not because you are doing it wrong or are broken; sometimes it is simply because that is either a technique that does not work for your specific body or because you need other knowledge and skills first before it can be useful. Many common grounding techniques are based on bringing you physically back to your body, which might not be the best experience depending on how your physical dysphoria presents.

Seeking out a trans-affirming therapist can allow you to work on the other symptoms while addressing gender when and where it's relevant. Finding a therapist who can work with all of your concerns simultaneously will allow you to do the work without having to know in advance what is connected or not. I will share a small secret of the trade: it's probably a big mess of complicated stuff (this is the official terminology) rather than nice linear threads that can be categorized as a "depression thing" over here and a "gender thing" over here and a "family thing" over there. Everything is interconnected and you don't need that information before seeking out a therapist; you can let them help you figure that out.

Unfortunately, there are many therapists who are not highly trained in working with trans clients and who attempt to address depression/anxiety/trauma first before wanting to address gender-specific concerns. This can be extremely detrimental when you are still in the process of exploring your gender identity, because while all of your mental health concerns are not going to be specific to gender, certainly some of them are. And wondering why none of the interventions for addressing your depression are working, when it is actually about the daily struggle of not being seen as who you are, could feel like a waste of everyone's time. If you can find someone who is able to see and address all the aspects of your identity, you will find the work much more fruitful and fulfilling.

How to assess a therapist

Finding the right therapist is going to depend on many factors, including how the healthcare system in your country works. For that reason, I will not go into specifics about how to do that.[38] Instead I will share how I think you can tell if you have found someone who can help you once you get in contact with options or have a first session.

You can assess your therapist by asking them a lot of questions. That's right, turn the tables on them, ask them about their relationship with their mother. I'm kidding...don't ask them about their mom, but do ask them questions. While the consultation or first session can be for them to gather information about you, you can and should gather information about them. You can ask them about how many trans people they have worked with and if they have specific training around gender/trans issues. You can ask them if they are familiar with certain terminology, or, if you are seeing them for a letter of referral to medical care, you can ask how they conduct the assessments and what will occur in those sessions.

Often people are afraid to ask therapists questions because they don't know what kinds of answers they should be looking to get.[39] I would say sometimes the answers to the questions are less important than how they respond and if it feels like they are open to discussing your concerns. If a therapist is dismissive or evasive or just makes you uncomfortable with the way they address things, they may not be the person for you. Your gut instinct is worth listening to, and if your interactions with a therapist continually feel off, then don't ignore it. This, of course, comes with the caveat that if you talk to many therapists and they all make you feel uncomfortable, this could just be an issue of therapy being inherently awkward and uncomfortable at the beginning, or that some aspect of being in therapy feels unsafe for a deeper reason (like trauma), or that maybe therapy is not the best option for you at this time. You can bring up your discomfort with a therapist and find out how they respond to your concerns. A good therapist can pivot and work with you in a way that feels collaborative and mutual.

Therapy is not the only option to receiving extra care and support. You may also be interested in peer support, coaching, psychiatry/medication, or other community or spiritual spaces. Therapy is certainly not the only route, and the most effective option is obviously the one that works for you and the one that you feel safe and comfortable in.

PART IV

Interpersonal

You've made it through the sections about your personal narratives of doubt, the historical context that some of those narratives appeared in, and how they may have impacted your mental health. Now we turn to the social and the communal. You're doing the work with yourself, but what does it look like to be a trans or questioning person around others? What does all of this mean for your relationships? Who exactly is your community and what do you need from them during this time?

CHAPTER 16

Labels: What Are They Good For?

Many people's first foray into the social element of their gender is trying to find the term to present themselves with. If gender is a conference, then your label is the "Hello My Name Is..." sticker. Fortunately, gender is not a conference.

Maybe you started reading this book asking yourself if you are trans, or nonbinary, or trans feminine nonbinary, or bigender, or a demi-boy, or genderfluid, or an old school butch, or something else entirely. (Here it is, here's the sentence that dates this book very firmly in 2023.) Maybe you pore over obscure pages on the internet looking for more terminology to define what it is you are. There is nothing wrong with that search for the correct word, but I also think people have an expectation for labels that isn't always helpful.

Labels exist to add to your experience instead of constricting it. A lot of people assume once they find the label then they will find the path. The label will tell you what to do and how to move forward. Unfortunately, labels do not have that specific power.

Labels can be incredibly beneficial. I think every queer and/ or trans person has a memory of finding a term and realizing that this was something that existed, and had a community, and that they were not alone. If the first time you learned the word "asexual" you were flooded with a feeling of relief and thought, *Oh, thank god, I'm not broken, there are other people like me*, you will likely feel gratitude toward that word. You may feel freed by that word. Labels can bring people community and take them out of their isolation. Labels point to whole other worlds that you may not have had access to before, and with that they bring a lot of hope.

But then you may find once you actually start connecting with that community that people break their identities down into more and more precise terms. Lesbians have mascs and femmes, studs and butches, stems and bois, Chapstick lesbians and lipstick lesbians, stone butches and soft butches. This can be overwhelming when you first enter a community, and you might struggle to know how to even begin to refine your own label. Of course, it is not required to refine the term further, but many people find it can be grounding to have a more specific label, and others can find the exercise a way to bond with other community members.

What eventually ends up happening for many is that their self-identifiers become so long and unwieldy (e.g. identifying as a power bottom high femme, except when the other person is more femme than you, in which case, you're more of a switch with some heavy daddy energy) that they become tired of going into a monologue each time it comes up. At that point you may see a lot of people forego their labels entirely ("labels are for soup cans" was once a common refrain in sections of the queer community) or start to identify with more general labels, like queer. This tendency toward foregoing labels often occurs after someone has found their community and they feel safe.

The labels never were meant to tell you who you are; they were simply meant to help you to explain who you are in different settings. You are probably much less likely to try to explain the daddy part of your sexuality to your grandmother and might just call yourself a lesbian around family. Then on a dating app, it is going to be a different story. Go wild. In each respective setting there are different needs being placed on these terms, and they are meant to convey different information in the conversation.

Gender labels are the same in that they do not define your actions; they are simply meant to explain and help you connect. But because the whole process of coming out as trans can feel so turbulent, people are desperate for any sense of structure. They want a map to guide them. Unknowingly they put all this pressure on the label to carry them through the unknown. But by doing that, sometimes you find a label that seems good enough, or at least better than what you had before, and when you try it on it feels constrictive.

Transition is a buffet and not a checklist. No part of this process is all or nothing. And labels do not necessitate actions, and actions do not necessitate certain labels. If you find out that you actually do want to go on hormones when you didn't think you did, that does not mean you have to stop identifying as nonbinary if you don't want to. And if it turns out that you identify with the label trans man, this doesn't suddenly mean you need to go on testosterone, grow a beard, have top surgery, post pictures of your top surgery on Instagram, have phalloplasty, and do all the "trans man things." This whole experience is a mix-and-match grab bag, and if you pick something up and it does not serve you, you can put it right back down. If your label starts to feel like an itchy, ill-fitting sweater, then take it off.

It is meant to serve you; otherwise what is the point of it? As we have seen, labels cannot be provided from outside sources. There is no therapist or doctor who can provide your label, but there is also no Queen of the Queers who knows you better than you know yourself.

Sometimes the easiest place to start is by allowing yourself to just be "not cis" for a while. If you are looking for answers in this book, it is probably pretty likely that you are not cis. Try holding that for a while. What if you allowed yourself to be guided by what you wanted rather than a word? The word could come in time, or maybe it wouldn't; maybe you will decide you do not need one. Maybe you will try some words and abandon some words. Maybe in twenty years someone will ask you how you define your gender and you will just sigh, not because you do not know but because you cannot be bothered to try to articulate it. That is all great. Your journey through labels will evolve because your journey will take you to new places. In other words, of course, the words you use to describe the path will change as the scenery around you does too. It is unlikely that one singular word will encompass who you are and were and will forever be.

If starting with a label feels like a barrier, then start somewhere else. There is absolutely no shame in that and it may be exactly what you need in order to progress to better understanding and further action. If it feels worthwhile to hold a label that you are not 100 percent sure of gently while you explore further, then you get to do that and no one can take that away from you.

Let's discuss three of the most common trans identity labels: nonbinary, trans woman, and trans man. Of course, these are not the only options available to you, and they certainly are not exclusive terms. As we discussed, it is possible to hold multiple identity labels, and even within these choices you may identify with more than one. These are simply three categories that much of the trans community falls within, and some of the context around what identifying with those labels might mean, and the external pressures and narratives that exist around them. I know I can't make you read anything but I believe there is interesting information in each of the chapters that follow, so even if you feel relatively comfortable and certain of your identity label, feel free to read the other chapters too.

CHAPTER 17

On Being a Nonbinary Person

As we discussed in Chapter 2, Internalizing Transphobia, society believes that there is no correct way to be nonbinary because being nonbinary already breaks one of the foundational rules of how to do gender correctly. Cisgender people do not have a vision of what a correct form of a nonbinary identity is because this is an oxymoron in their eyes. There is no script for being nonbinary. (This doesn't mean that cisgender people do not have standards for nonbinary presentations that make them feel more comfortable, but that is far from accepting the validity of the identity itself.) This lack of a script is a blessing and a curse. It is a blessing because how can you be doing something wrong if no one knows what you're doing? And it is a curse because how can you be doing it right if no one knows what you're doing? Binary trans people can at least check against the notes of other binary trans people and in a worst-case scenario look to cis men and women to get some guidance or examples (which they hopefully take with a grain of salt; cis people are not the experts on womanhood or manhood either). Most cultures currently don't acknowledge the existence of more than two genders, and that makes this all feel like uncharted territory for many nonbinary people.

It is commonly believed that nonbinary identities are new or a fad. Sometimes they are considered a Western invention or what happens when a society is too permissive. This is far from the truth. There have been nonbinary people (or what have been considered third, fourth, and even fifth genders) in many cultures, on all continents, and in all of human history. A history of colonialism has violently disconnected many people from the history of genders outside the binary even within their own cultures.

In 1990, "two-spirit" was created to be an umbrella term during the Third Annual Inter-tribal Native American, First Nations, Gay and Lesbian American Conference. The conference had dozens of tribes who had hundreds of terms for genders outside the binary, and the term "two-spirit" was a way to both create an umbrella term and reclaim the language and the narrative for themselves. The creation of this term fought back against a colonialist history that has sought to erase these experiences and force them into a European, Christian understanding of gender and sexuality. Two-spirit people were traditionally given special roles with their community, and in many tribes, those roles were spiritual and revered. The term, of course, is only to be used by Native people, but it started a conversation around a history of nonbinary identities in North America that had been previously unknown to many people.

Like much of trans history, the accounts of nonbinary lives have been hidden or destroyed. Frequently nonbinary people have been told that their identities are not even real. When these identities are acknowledged, it is common that nonbinary people often have been forced to fit into cis spaces or binary trans spaces. Nonbinary people are often seen as not cis enough, or not trans enough, and then not taken seriously by either group. Being nonbinary is either considered a purely aesthetic choice that is related to androgyny or it is considered being "trans-lite." This leads to a belief that nonbinary people have it much easier and that nonbinary people could revert to a more cis-passing identity and be fine (much like the "straight-passing" narrative of bisexuality: bisexual people are seen to have straight-passing privilege, rather than an obligation to hide aspects of their identity in order to be safe and respected). This is not true, and nonbinary identities are not lesser versions of binary genders.

Being nonbinary is not a place on a scale where if you don't want enough elements of transition, you are labeled nonbinary. A nonbinary person can want just as many social, legal, and medical parts of transition as a binary trans person, and, of course, they can want none (just like a binary person can). Hopefully it goes without saying, but the only thing that determines whether someone is nonbinary or not is whether they identify outside the gender binary. That is the one and only criterion. And "outside of" is quite a location. Some consider their nonbinary identity to be in between binary genders; some do not feel they can describe it in relation to two points. The location "outside of" is infinite. If someone describes where they live as "outside of Los Angeles," they could mean a few miles south of the county lines in Orange County, or they could mean in Peru, or they could mean on the International Space Station. While it would be an interesting way of answering the question at hand for some of those options, it may feel like the only way to answer when everyone walks around asking, "Where in Los Angeles do you live?" If you don't live there, what do you say? "I don't, I live outside of Los Angeles." By asking someone if they are a man or a woman, the answers become limited and strangely framed because they presuppose the answer is limited to the binary. But there's a whole world outside of Los Angeles.

Even for those who confidently know that they are non-binary, this presupposing of the binary can become a mental block. Much of the world is built firmly upon the foundation of two genders. The internalized voice of not being nonbinary enough can be blaringly loud, when not only are you comparing yourself with cis and other trans experiences but also the external narrative says your experience is made up. It is nearly impossible not to have that self-doubt when you are questioned and challenged every step of the way. The ability to arrive at an inner confidence in a nonbinary identity requires a great deal of strength, but maybe more practically, it requires the ability to drown out those external and internal voices. It asks you to prioritize your own voice and make your mind and body quiet enough so you can hear what it is trying to tell you.

Many nonbinary people doubt their process because they cannot envision the destination. Hopefully it is more than apparent that if knowing the destination was required for any trans person, then no one would make it. Stumbling around is part of the game. But identifying as nonbinary can be a temporary stopover for some and it can be a permanent identity for others. In much the same way that some people come out as bisexual before they come out as gay or lesbian, some people do come out as nonbinary before they come out as a binary trans person. In the same way, that does not mean that bisexuals don't exist. Bisexuals definitely exist. The existence of people who needed the label of bisexual as a stepping stone to their gay identity does not invalidate the people who are bisexual their whole lives. The part that is usually frustrating is that you can't really know which one you are until you take those steps and see if it's where you land or where you make a pit stop. The biggest problem occurs when people decide they know exactly where they are going and don't allow themselves to continue to learn and evolve once they've reached what they believe is the finish line. Many try to promise their loved ones that they definitely won't go on hormones, or definitely won't change their name, or definitely won't ever need their kids to start calling them something other than "Dad." This often does not go according to plan, and then that person has to go back and tell everyone that actually they were mistaken.

Again, it is not that every trans and nonbinary person goes on to do those things, simply that feeling the need to aggressively reassure someone that you will never do those things often has more to do with reassuring yourself that you will not pass a certain threshold of change. Usually the one you are trying to convince is yourself. You have begun the bargaining phase of, *I can be this much trans, but any more trans than that is out of the question.* Try your best not to do that. Do not limit your future based on what you know about yourself now, and do not create lines of how much transition is allowed and how much space your gender gets to take up. Try not to get caught up in wondering if where you are is where you will be forever, and instead allow yourself to be available when your mind and body have information to share with you. Day one of identifying as nonbinary is never going to look like day 893, and that is a wonderful thing. (And if day 894 brings a new label, that is also a wonderful thing.) Give your feelings the weight they deserve and surround yourself with others who will too, because it is unlikely that the world at large will be able to offer you what you need. Your very existence is outside their understanding.

CHAPTER 18

On Being a Trans Woman

S exism and transmisogyny[40] make coming out and living as a trans woman a more complex experience than the experience of more masculine-presenting nonbinary people and trans masculine people. Unfortunately, trans feminine bodies are more closely scrutinized, and gender roles for women are more restrictive and socially enforced.

Looking back at some of the most well-known early stories of medical transition, you will hear about people like Lili Elbe (of *The Danish Girl* fame), Christine Jorgensen, and, more recently, Caitlyn Jenner. I think there are number of reasons historically why you will see trans women before you see trans men, and one is certainly the cultural shock value and how this is considered a transgression of the foundational rules of gender and power.

Christine Jorgensen became famous in the US for her gender-affirming surgeries, and the headline Americans saw in 1952 was "Ex-GI Becomes Blonde Beauty." The story gained interest because of the cultural shock that someone as "manly" as a soldier could actually be a transgender woman. The story captured mainstream attention in a way that many trans stories in the United States had not before, and it tapped into many questions that the public had about gender. Many saw trans women as abandoning their male privilege, and this was a large piece of what was seen as pathological. Many cis people were asking themselves why someone would abandon their social power unless they were mentally ill. Not only does this say a lot about how privilege has been understood, but it certainly says a lot about how the gender hierarchy was seen as an unchangeable, objective truth. People emphatically believed that men are on top of the hierarchy, and they should be, and that this is the natural order (of course, many still believe this today). To abandon your supposed birthright at the top of the social order is incomprehensible to most people.

This is not actually the trans experience, but it was and is how many cis people view it. The narrative has been that trans women have gender-based privilege and then lose it as they transition, and that trans men did not have gender-based privilege and then gain it as they transition. While that is the experience of some trans people, others find it is too simplistic to be a useful account. Factors like race, size, physical and mental ability, and even the age at which you began your transition are going to affect how people treat and treated you. Privilege and oppression are not on/off switches where you either have it completely or you have none at all, and there is no experience of separating your race from your gender when you cannot experience your life with your race and gender as separate pieces of the whole.

Many trans women have challenged the idea that the experience of a closeted trans woman is going to show up the same as male privilege. Again, there are many factors to take into account, so it is impossible to explain one monolithic experience of trans women, but many trans women don't identify with a story where they had the same kind of male privilege pre-transition as their cis male peers. The presumption that trans feminine people had male privilege rests on the assumption that they were seen as boys or men before and have all the access and privilege of a boy or man until they come out, at which time they supposedly lose this privilege. But there are a number of questions that must be asked to make that determination: Do people see you as doing manhood, boyhood, or masculinity correctly before you come out? If you are seen as doing this role incorrectly, do you still receive privilege? Will you be shunned and shamed for not wielding your privilege correctly? Will your gender be policed and corrected until you perform it according to other people's expectations? Perhaps having a male name on a resume will provide you with an advantage in job hunting; will that advantage continue once you are hired and then your masculinity is deemed insufficient according to the expectations of your employer? Even in that scenario, you and the employer would not need to know that you are trans for your experience to be different from cis male employees. There are many examples where the experience of a closeted trans feminine person is not going to be identical to either a cis man or a cis woman. By assuming that trans people are going to have experiences identical to cis people before coming out, we are again placing binaries on the trans experience that were never meant to include trans people in the first place.

The narrative of trans feminine people having male privilege has been criticized by many trans theorists and again seems to be based on a cis, and therefore external, perspective. It is not a narrative that takes the necessary nuance and subtlety into account and is not everyone's lived experience. A story where a boy becomes a woman is easier for cis people to understand, but it is not the way most trans women tell their own stories. This can lead to trans people formulating their stories according to the expectations of cis people, but perhaps more specifically, according to the limitations of the cis imagination. The watering down of trans stories will never serve us the way we hope it will. Allowing the community to have a true diversity of experience, rather than forcing people to tell their stories according to a certain narrative, will only be a benefit to the trans community. Trans people live intersectional lives that deserve to be spoken about without limitation.

Scrutiny of trans feminine bodies

Trans feminine bodies are scrutinized to a much greater extent than trans masculine bodies, partially for the reason that all women's bodies are scrutinized to a greater extent than men's, but also because trans feminine bodies can be considered a threat.

Straight cis male culture is one that does a great deal of work to manage the threat of appearing gay. You might recognize this as "no-homo" culture. Certainly not every cis straight man is threatened to the same degree, but boys and men, as a whole, disseminate information about how to protect their heterosexual reputations. This process begins very young, often before a boy has a chance to understand the implications of these messages around gender and sexuality.

Combined with narratives that say trans women are secretly just men or used to be men, this fuels all kinds of no-homo panic that then becomes scrutiny of trans women's bodies.

Straight men teach each other to be wary around women who are too tall, have broad shoulders, or who have an Adam's apple. The goal is to avoid being accidentally attracted to what they deem to be a man, because this would threaten their entire identity as straight and masculine and macho. Sadly this is not just an unfortunate belief held by men with fragile egos; it has also made its way into legal strategy, where lawyers argue that their client became violent against a trans person because they were tricked. Even more unfortunately, these kinds of defenses have been successful in many cases. Eight states have banned what are colloquially called gay/trans panic defenses. This defense strategy claims that it is justified to become panicked and respond with violence if you did not know the person you were interacting with (generally sexually) is transgender.

Much of the gay panic of straight men comes down to the power of the penis in our cultural mythology. Penises are seen as threatening, and two penises in a hookup supposedly is gay. In order for a cis straight man to maintain his masculinity in a no-homo society, any contact with other penises must be avoided at all costs.

This is not how masculinity was always defined and pro-tected. The ancient Greeks put more stock in who was the top and who was the bottom to assess masculinity, rather than the gender of the person. This is not to say that that is the correct way to view these gender and power dynamics, simply that they have not been stagnant across history. A great deal has now changed, where now two men in a threesome with a woman can reassure themselves that "it's not gay if the balls don't touch." In this culture there are strange rituals around ensuring that experiences stay safe and as not-gay as possible. To most people in the twenty-first century, gender is a critical factor and penises doubly so.

Trans feminine people can also be subjected to a message that states that they are sexual predators. Particularly when trans feminine people are attracted to women, they are said to be exploiting a power dynamic for their own gain. We know this is not true and that queer trans feminine people as a group are no more likely to be predators than anyone else. In fact, the opposite is far more likely to be true. Trans people are an extremely vulnerable population. It is much more likely that cis abusers will seek out trans people to victimize than vice versa.[41]

Regardless of that research, it is easy for those narratives to be internalized and create shame and guilt for those trans feminine people who are attracted to women. It feels like there is little space for the sort of softness or sweetness that is often afforded to cisgender queer women by other cisgender queer women. (It is not something that is commonly afforded to them by anyone else, considering straight men are usually too busy fetishizing or objectifying queer women.) If society does not allow trans women to be women, then it continues to place the huge burden of male lechery onto them. Trans women are said to bring the same kinds of dynamics into a relationship that a man would. This is not true and is based on the falsehood that deep down trans women are really men or have the power of men. There is no combination of genders and sexualities, or body parts and orientations, that is inherently predatory. There are simply long histories of transphobia that have been weaponized against the community in various ways and that get turned into internalized doubts. Even without being able to articulate how these social dynamics function, it is common to be plagued with a vague feeling that pursuing an interest in women is not allowed for whatever reason. This mutates into a self-doubt that makes it harder to pursue relationships with women, which makes the feeling of "maybe I am a creep" louder, which makes it harder to pursue the relationships and so on. There is a vicious cycle that keeps trans feminine people from breaking the mental cycle and experiencing the truth of a queer relationship like that. And the truth of that queer relationship looks nothing like what society claims it is: the lecherous, oppressive dynamic of a man-pretending-to-be-a-woman trying to lower the defenses of a woman in order to trick her into a relationship. These relationships have the power to be just as open, sweet, kind, authentic, and loving as any other relationship.

Cisgender men are the primary architects for many of these narratives, but also some cisgender women work hard to protect against the supposed threat of the penis. Trans exclusionary radical feminists (or TERFs)[42] believe that trans women are interlopers who are trying to gain access to women's spaces. TERF ideology has stemmed out of parts of second-wave feminism and continues mostly with second-wave feminists (although they continue to try to influence new generations of women and government policy). Phrases like "womyn-born-womyn"[43] have come to be covers for the kind of transphobia that seems to believe that having a penis is a threat to women's spaces, and in fact *ever* having had a penis is a threat to women's spaces. Sometimes TERF ideology is presented as if it is the logical conclusion to certain objective truths. Or in other words, TERFs claim they have examined all the facts and it is merely a coincidence that the conclusion always ends in excluding trans people. If you try to nail down if they have issues with penises or if they have issues with "male privilege," you will find that it is slippery and ever changing. The concerns change and it is hard to locate what the foundational problem is.

It can be hard to know if what they claim to be the threat is actually what they see as the threat. Many TERFs will go on tirades about the threat of the penis, and when you point out that of course some trans women have vaginas, another problem arises. The goalposts are moved, and you are stuck in another debate about another supposed threat. The goalposts will always move because, whether the threat is being deemed gay (in the case of cis men), or penises, or the lingering threat of a no-longer-present penis, or supposed maleness, or living a life of "male privilege," it is impossible to know what the foundational concern is. If these people were honest, we could expect to hear that the underlying problem is "trans women are not really women." There is nothing deeper to be understood, and they don't deserve the kinds of good-faith arguments they consistently try to demand from the unwitting victims of their rhetoric. That is because the foundational problem is that they do not like trans people. After you come to terms with that, it is much easier to see why all the outcomes are transphobic. It is because transphobia is the foundation, so transphobia will always be the outcome.

What is truly impressive is that these sorts of anti-trans narratives are so deeply ingrained that they have looped back around and started to be weaponized against cisgender women. Caster Semenya is a female Olympic runner who came under public scrutiny for having testosterone levels deemed too high to compete. The International Association of Athletics Federations require women with too high testosterone (according to their standards) to take medication to lower the levels. This caused the media and the public to speculate if Semenya actually had an intersex condition or was "really a man." Semenya has never publicly discussed her medical history and is under no obligation to, but others saw her as having an unfair advantage in her sport and felt the need to keep her naturally produced testosterone in check. She is not the only female athlete who has been accused of really being a man. Any time a woman competes and is seen as too fast or too strong or too muscular, there is subtle or not-so-subtle speculation about the "reality" of her body and medical history. It does not even need to be based on any evidence, and it rarely aspires to provide any evidence aside from the outraged belief that a woman could not accomplish such a feat. When people say that Serena Williams was born a man, it is hard to say how many people actually believe it and how many are just using it to punish a woman they see as stepping outside of the limitations they have placed on women. The rhetoric that intends to restrict trans women becomes so common that it affects cis women as well.

Both of the examples given here are Black women, and it is easy to find that these objections are more likely to be specifically aimed at Black women. Racism factors in strongly and becomes what has been dubbed "misogynoir."[44] Trans and intersex bodies[45] have created so much panic that all women are held to the same intense scrutiny and examination. Being tall or fast or even having high levels of testosterone does not mean anything about the reality of a person's gender, which means any woman outside a very narrow view of what is an acceptable woman gets caught up in the inquisition.

Is it that grim?

By focusing specifically on the experiences of trans women, a lot can appear very grim. History has not been kind, and the present is not yet a place that feels free of threats. Change is happening rapidly, but no one can guarantee an experience that is free of bias and bigotry. This makes it hard to see why transitioning or presenting as a woman could be worth it.

Many people use that as a reason to put off their transition or to take it off the table entirely. They fear they will not be able to handle the awkwardness, stigma, or sexism, and they assume it is better to continue along with the level of relative comfort they may have at the moment. Or in other words, it feels better to deal with the devil they know than the one they don't. And yet if that was the exclusive reality of what trans women had to look forward to, then no one would go down a path of transitioning (or if they did, we would expect to see much higher rates of detransition).

These narratives can all contribute to the way that you move through the world and the way that people sometimes experience your identity, but they are not the totality of the experience. If you are a trans woman, then you are a trans woman, and there is no path of peace and serenity that exists through avoidance and not embracing that.[46] That can sound like a begrudging inevitability for many people on the side of pre-transition. It can sound like a doomed fate. That is because until you begin your own process of embracing it you cannot experience all the joy that will come, only the anticipatory fear. Joy and calm and a sense of rightness come from an embodied experience.

There are so many trans women living a life that is more satisfied and fulfilled than they thought possible, and there is no reason why you would be excluded from that.

It can feel impossible to know the responsible position on the spectrum from paranoia to naivety. Is it better to expect the worst or is it better to naively assume that nothing will go wrong? There is no objectively true answer about what level of risk you can expect, but as we have seen, living in the anxiety only creates an anticipatory pain that demands to be experienced over and over again in your own mind.

Perhaps the most useful way to challenge this uncertainty is by having community. Connecting with other trans women who have experienced both the good and the bad allows connection, commiseration, strategies for addressing danger, and, most importantly, hope. It is too difficult to experience these anxieties in isolation, and a community reinforces the power you already have. As we know, the difficulties of being trans don't stem from the internal experience of gender but from a society that doesn't allow trans lives to be joyful. We must find our communities that accept and celebrate the joy.

CHAPTER 19

On Being a Trans Man

Trans men have historically been more in the shadows. For a long time, it was believed that there were fewer trans men than trans women. Recent research shows that the numbers are relatively even. There is not an enormous disparity where there are far more trans women than trans men, but there was an enormous disparity in terms of who was counted. This was likely because it has been easier for trans men to live stealth (or to pass as cis), due to the signals society keeps an eye out for. Which is to say, generally most people are not going to take as much note of a short man compared with a tall woman. Most people are not going to scrutinize a man with wider hips compared with a woman with wider shoulders. This has little to do with identities and bodies and more to do with what our society has determined to be acceptable diversity of bodies and what that means. There is a larger range of acceptable male bodies than there are acceptable female bodies.

It is always difficult to determine which history can be claimed as "trans history." Particularly in situations where historians have shown that a "woman lived life as a man," there will always be debate about if this was a decision this person made in order to have an easier life and gain rights and privileges that weren't afforded to women at the time or if it was due to the person's gender identity, or if it was some combination of gaining social power plus factors of sexuality or gender. There are also arguments about whether it is fair to view historical figures through a modern lens. Is it fair and accurate to look at individuals who lived many years ago and call them transgender and use the terms of gender identity that are used in the twenty-first century?

The life of Billy Tipton, a jazz musician who lived as male until his death in 1989, is one debated case. Some scholars and historians attempt to categorize him as a woman who lived as a man, some categorize him as a lesbian, and others consider him a trans man. One trans scholar, Jason Cromwell, states:

> Billy Tipton's life speaks for itself. The male privileges that accrue from living as a man do not justify spending fifty years living in fear, hiding from loved ones, taking extreme measures to make sure that no one knows what their body is or looks like, and then dying from a treatable medical condition (a bleeding ulcer). When someone like Tipton dies or is discovered, they are discounted as having been "not real men" or "unreal men." Despite having lived for years as men, the motivations of these individuals are read as being wrought of socioeconomic necessity or the individuals are considered to be lesbians. Does this mean that "anatomy is not destiny" while one is alive but "anatomy is destiny" after death?[47]

I have to agree, and all the signs point to this being another instance of trans lives and history being misunderstood and erased. But it is unlikely these questions will ever be answered

definitively without any discovery of how these historical figures described themselves in their own words. There will always
be debate, and there will always be different modern groups
attempting to claim the lives of people who cannot speak for
themselves for their own narratives or political aims. It is safe
to say, even if only some of the "women living as men" would
consider themselves transgender men today, some percentage
of them certainly would. We will never have firm numbers and
we may never know exactly which ones, but we can be sure that
this likely occurred far more often than we will ever get to know.

Society believes that people who aspire to greater power and
status (i.e. masculinity) are acting logically. Society says, *Why
wouldn't a woman want to be a man? Who doesn't want to be a man?
Men get all the good shit.* This is a somewhat fair point in that, yes,
when you are dealing with sexism and misogyny, then being a
woman is a huge hassle at best. An idea like Freud's penis envy
tends to make more sense when you take it as women desiring
the social privilege that men receive (rather than Freud's theory
that all women are literally envious of the penis and want one
for themselves).[48]

And with a long history of theorists and clinicians pontificat-
ing about how of course anyone would love to be a man, there
is then a social space for trans men to exist where their desires
are not immediately pathologized to the same degree that trans
women's desires are. Within this framework it is very logical to
understand why you would want all the cool cash and prizes that
come from being a man, whereas, in the case of a trans woman,
why would you give that up?

In the DSM-IV, the diagnosis for gender identity disorder
said that the diagnosis could not be given due to desiring any

advantages of the opposite sex. And while it's not stated explicitly, we can only assume this advantage would be male privilege (unless I am unaware of some other major cultural advantages of being openly transgender). This language reinforced the fact that this was supposedly a common motivation for transition, and a patient must be assessed to confirm that they were not some sort of elaborate con artist, or poor fool who believed transition would open up perks in life.

You and I both know that this is not what motivates people to transition. It is not about wanting male privilege so badly that you decide to live life as a man. (And obviously again in the case of a trans woman, it is not about being mentally ill and wanting to give up the birthright of male privilege.) But that can also be a doubt that can take root in the minds of many trans men: *What if I just hate being a woman because of sexism? What if I have internalized societal misogyny and have so thoroughly convinced myself that being a man would be better that I have started to believe I am one?* I can promise you that is not what happened. If that was what made people transgender men or trans masculine people, there would be a whole lot more of us. There are billions of women on this earth experiencing varying levels of sexism and misogyny, and the vast majority of them do not decide to give up on being a woman. If the internalized misogyny theory held up, then we would also see far more trans men than trans women. But we don't. We see very equal numbers of people assigned male at birth, and assigned female at birth, transitioning.

It is important to note that while there is often space for tomboys and other masculine-presenting women in many cultures, obviously trans men are subjected to transphobia too. What that often means is that there is an invisible line where someone is allowed to explore masculinity up to a point and then it becomes unacceptable. Generally, that line is when someone begins to identify as trans, wants to move through the world permanently as a man, or wishes to alter their body through surgery or hormones. It can be very jarring for one's gender identity to be mostly ignored or seen as a quirk throughout childhood and then for it to suddenly be seen as unacceptable or threatening once it begins to seem too advanced to be a trait of a cisgender person. And more confusingly still, feminine trans men will generally have an entirely different trajectory than a masculine-presenting trans man, where their femininity will be seen as in line with their assumed cis female identity until it isn't, and the swift and drastic change in feedback is a shock to everyone involved.

Passing the invisible line

With all other factors being equal, men do have more privilege in our society. And while that can be a benefit in mainstream cisgender society, many trans people have found their home in queer spaces and community. Some parts of the queer community have worked very hard to distance themselves from the rules, pressures, and influence of the cisgender and heterosexual mainstream. For those trans masculine people who may have identified as butch, or who found comfort in spaces of queer women, any step toward identifying with manhood can feel extremely complicated.

Narratives of betraying the community of women, or becoming the enemy, are born out of those same second-wave feminist/

TERF beliefs that we discussed in Chapter 18. Some second-wave feminists felt strongly that distancing themselves from men was important both personally and politically. As previously mentioned, this was weaponized by TERFs against trans women who were seen as interlopers, but it was also weaponized against trans masculine people, and sometimes even butches. There was an us versus them mentality that became more hardened the more those cultural and political fights raged on. This is often the case when an oppressed group starts to get more public attention for their fight for rights—the oppressed community has to reinforce the strength of their much smaller community, which often includes being very careful about who is on their side and who is able to be trusted.

Unfortunately, this meant that people who were not trying to sabotage the feminist movement were still included in the group that was seen as the enemy. The definition of who was safe and on their side became increasingly narrow, and almost all trans people were seen as suspect. Some believed that anyone who had a penis (or honestly, anyone who had ever had a penis) were either interlopers or too close to maleness/male privilege, and those who aspired to anything more masculine/ closer to maleness were also the enemy. This excludes almost every trans person, if not all trans people. Trans people were either too masculine before, or had too masculine a body before, or they do now. And again at this stage of TERF ideology the foundation is transphobia, and that effect is intentional. But even people who do not identify as TERFs have been affected by this history and the reactions and strategies put in place to protect the community.

Because there was a large group of lesbians and queer women

in those spaces, they have brought those ideas with them into present-day queer spaces. Many queer women continue a kind of misandry that sometimes is hard to know whether is joking or serious. It has become almost embedded into the culture of queer women's spaces whether it is directly addressed or merely indirectly joked about. Many trans masculine people feel there is an unspoken line of transition where they will no longer be welcome in certain communities, parties, or friend groups. The implied narrative is that any gender is good except being a man. There are many trans people who will easily call themselves a guy, or a dude, or a boy, or any number of words, but they will never use the word man. Of course, no one is required to call themselves any specific word or label and each individual is the only person who will be able to determine if they are a man or not, but the careful tiptoeing around the language of manhood is certainly affected by this history that states you can be masculine but not too masculine. People begin to believe that there is an invisible line drawn and because no one can tell you exactly where that line is located, it is best to stay a safe distance away from it.

There is a lot to say about this, but first and foremost it holds lots of people back from feeling as if transition is even something they can consider. If you go from feeling completely isolated in cisgender heterosexual society to feeling as if you have a home and a community in queer women's spaces, then you are not going to give that up easily. The reality is that that community may not have to be something you give up, but there is no way to know how your specific community will react to your transition until it happens. For those trans masculine people who are primarily attracted to women, it often appears that there is a false binary of either transitioning and having to return to the cisgender heterosexual world or not transitioning and staying in the queer one. The reality is not so black and white, and every person gets to determine what elements of their queer identity are important to them, who their friends are, and what kind of events they want to go to. Instead it feels like they must beg for permission to continue to be seen as a part of the group. This is not the case, and people who see you as betraying your community by being your true self have their own issues to work through and may be affected by a historical narrative that they do not even fully understand themselves.

Being a man and/or having a penis or desiring either of those things is not inherently harmful. Trans masculine people have the ability to create a new and less toxic form of masculinity should they choose to take that opportunity. And that is indeed an opportunity, although it can feel like a burden at times. It is a great benefit to you and to the world to accept it as an opportunity. Toxic masculinity is taught, and even cisgender men can unlearn it. But trans masculine people who have been able to see it from multiple perspectives have an incredible ability to have their authentic identity and not bring toxic masculinity as a carry-on. Separating masculinity and toxicity can be done; they do not have to go hand in hand.

Conditional privilege

For those trans men who do gain privilege by transition (this is, of course, dependent on race), perhaps the easiest way to explain it is to say that it's conditional. When a trans man moves through public spaces perceived as a cisgender man, he gains the safety of being ignored. But that safety is dependent on being perceived as not just a man but as a cisgender man. There is a public-facing safety that is dependent upon no one having any access to any further details about his past or his body. I've heard it said that trans men have privilege in being men and are oppressed for being trans. This statement sounds clear and plausible, but in my own experience I haven't found it possible to pull those two aspects of my identity apart. I am not transgender over here and a man over there. While there may be a newfound ability to walk through a dark alley at night, the threat of what happens if someone has to do a background check, run a credit check, look at a driver's license that hasn't been updated, do a medical exam, have access to medical history, or see any evidence that this man is not cisgender remains ever present. When you start to take into account that people spend most of their time at home and at work, the impact of landlords, banks, employers, and corporations having personal details of our lives is not negligible. Even the time spent outside of the home or workplace usually requires carrying around a wallet full of identification and payment cards. Every trans person exists with some bureaucratic record of their past, and other people having access to those records can lead to very real harm. The effect might decrease over time, with greater ability to blend in as cis, or more correct identification, but this does little to soothe questions about the kinds of emergencies that could strip away that veneer of safety, such as: *What happens if I am pulled over and they do a pat down? What happens if I'm in an accident and have to be taken to the hospital in an ambulance?*

It makes sense that people want a simplified statement about how privilege functions. It is much easier to say that trans men have privilege and trans women don't, but that statement takes away the nuance of actual trans experience. There are ways to hold that trans men and trans women have very different experiences without claiming that being a trans man shields someone from transphobic violence and oppression.

CHAPTER 20

Relationships

Whether you begin the process of questioning your gender while single or in romantic/sexual relationship(s), the idea of how transition will affect those current or future relationships is difficult to anticipate. As we have discussed, we experience our genders relationally as well as personally, and romantic relationships are often where those relational dynamics feel most fraught and vulnerable.

In a pre-existing relationship, it can feel like you are making a choice for yourself or for the relationship. The needs of each party may feel at odds. What happens if you transition and it is a problem for your partner? What happens if you do not transition in order to make your partner happy or more comfortable and it becomes a problem for you? The more emotional intimacy and time investment there is in a relationship, the larger and more insurmountable those questions feel. Many people put off transitioning well after they know that it is something they need for themselves because it feels so terrifying to find out the answer to whether their relationship will survive the drastic change.

Sometimes it feels like you can put off getting an answer to a question if you never really ask it. The answer is too terrifying to know, so by not asking it you never have to find out. This is just a mental loophole that is not as protective as it feels. If, as your brain begins to near asking the question, you think, *It's fine, it's fine, it's fine, it's fine,* and your brain tries to distract you from fully articulating it (even inside your own mind), then you are terrified of knowing the answer. But any question worth asking is worth getting an answer to, and whether you want to focus on the question or not, you have already asked it. The avoidance of it means it already exists and cannot be un-asked. It is worth answering in itself, but you also deserve to know the answer so you can move forward.

If the answer to "If I transition, will we break up?" is yes, then you deserve to know that, just as much as if the answer is no. Because while one answer may be heartbreaking, it is information that will serve you and your future. It will perhaps allow you the space to determine what you need from future partners and the ability to seek it out. Should that happen, it will open up a new stage of grief. This grief is navigated and survivable like all the others, but the pain of familial rejection and rejection by chosen family can tap into separate feelings of abandonment.

The loss of a significant partner can feel like the loss of a person who was a refuge from other forms of bias and oppression. If, for example, your family or workplace was homophobic, your partner may have been the person who understood and supported you when you experienced that homophobia. That feeling of support is an extremely hard thing to lose, especially when that person was a part of your life during a foundational time in your process of self-discovery. Your partner may have felt like the one person on your team when it was the two of you against the world. When that is the case, asking the terrifying question is all the more difficult.

What happens if you feel that this is the only person who will ever love you and transition would make you even more difficult to love or find desirable? These fears need to be discussed, but it is important to know that they are not a guarantee of how you will be treated or your chances of finding love and respect. There are many people who will not use these fears to manipulate you into accepting less than you deserve.

Intimate partner violence

These are scary thoughts, and they may not be based on anything other than fear, but there are times when the partners of trans people explicitly or implicitly utilize those kinds of messages to manipulate their partner's actions. This functions to make transgender people more susceptible to emotional abuse (and other forms of intimate partner violence) than cisgender people. Dynamics of reliance or codependency coupled with the many intersections of other forms of oppression make trans people a particularly vulnerable target for abusers. One study showed that as many as 54 percent of trans adults have experienced at least one form of intimate partner violence at some point.[49] While many people think of intimate partner violence as physical or sexual abuse, it also includes financial abuse, isolation abuse, identity abuse, and emotional abuse.

How do those lesser-known forms of abuse function?

- Financial abuse can be either that the abuser demands that the survivor pay for expenses or that the abuser makes decisions or denies the survivor access to financial resources.
- Isolation abuse is the act of keeping someone isolated

from friends, family, or community in order to have more
control over them.

- Identity abuse has been broken into three categories of
denigrating identity, denying identity, and manipulating
identity:
  - Denigrating identity is when an abuser tells a trans
person that no one will ever love them for being
trans or uses slurs or other language to disparage
the survivor's trans identity.
  - Denying identity is essentially what it sounds like:
when an abuser refuses to acknowledge or accept a
trans person's gender.
  - Manipulating identity is when an abuser controls
how the survivor transitions or acts, or compliments/
criticizes the survivor in ways that attempt to control their expression of gender.
- Emotional abuse can be anything from manipulation,
to blaming, lying, name-calling, re-writing history and
so on.

Because of the precarious social position of trans people, and
the fact that many of these styles of abuse are not always well
known as abuse, trans people are sometimes left wondering if
this is the only kind of relationship they can expect to have.
Or worse still, that these are completely normal dynamics and
simply what a relationship is meant to be like. When a trans
person's internalized doubt or shame couples with the abusive
messages from another person, there is a perfect storm of risk.
The reality is that no one deserves to be treated this way and
anyone who makes you feel as if your trans identity is something

that they are merely putting up with, or that they are doing you a favor by accepting this part of yourself, is not a partner who loves and respects you the way they are claiming to.

Even the healthiest relationships may have an adjustment period when one person transitions. A cis partner may need time to understand what this means for the relationship, their sexuality, and their identity. Sometimes after the adjustment period the relationship comes out stronger and healthier on the other side. Sometimes it is a time when it is discovered that the relationship will not last and two people may go their separate ways or need to drastically redefine the relationship. There is nothing wrong with this, assuming that the cis partner does not blame or fault the trans partner's process of self-discovery for any conflict that might arise. There must be a foundation of respect throughout all these stages, and no trans person is required to sit through a partner's resentment, disdain, or disgust at their newly explored gender identity.

Disclosure in new relationships

When it comes to new connections, the question of when to disclose your trans identity is one that every trans person on a dating app has struggled with. Due to transphobic bias, the burden is placed on the trans person to determine when and how to bring up this topic. The conversation will almost certainly be relevant at some stage of dating or hooking up, but the details of what needs to be said could vary greatly depending on the kind of connection and the stage of your transition. This might be a conversation that needs to occur in order to determine sexual boundaries or to determine if the relationship has long-term potential. Unfortunately or fortunately, there is no correct answer to this question and it will depend on a number of personal factors. Generally, people choose one of a few different times to disclose their trans identity. The first is completely up front, where the disclosure may be written in the dating profile itself, or in the first couple of messages of a chat. A second commonly chosen time is in the first few dates, or potentially after someone has determined that there is at least some chemistry or connection after meeting in person. And finally, it may be before the relationship becomes physical or sexual.

Each option has its pros and cons, but in each instance the primary concern to consider is safety. Many people prefer options where they do not disclose in person because it is physically the safest option and there is no threat of violence. It is still extremely risky to disclose a trans identity to someone in person, and even when it does not result in physical violence, there are still many ways the situation can be emotionally dangerous.

The option of disclosing up front is arguably the safest option, but many people do not choose it because they fear they are limiting their dating pool. They are concerned that if their Tinder profile says that they are trans, people will immediately reject them and not try to get to know them better. This is certainly something that happens. Picture-based dating apps are breeding grounds for implicit bias. Yet it is worth considering what limiting one's dating pool truly means. If, for the sake of an example, there were 2000 people who met your age, location, and gender/sexuality parameters on an app, would that mean that you actually had 2000 available suitors? Probably not. Chances are you would reject some people based on their political beliefs, or their looks, or their rudeness, or a thousand other factors, and those 2000 people would do the same to you. Some would reject you for legitimate reasons like the fact that you are in different stages in life, and others for more arbitrary reasons like "I can't date anyone who likes Top 40 pop music." The idea of the full 2000 people being available and good matches is a fantasy. (Not to mention the number of people who are on dating apps and not actually interested in dating, but that is a different discussion.) The initial number of possible matches is a fantasy of possibility, and as we know, fantasies of possibility are hard to abandon.

Perhaps by putting that you are trans in your profile the number of interested people is immediately reduced to 1000 people or even 200 people. It is hard to be rejected for something that is not within your control, but that means that those are people who are real possibilities, rather than the fantasy. This saves the time and misery of talking to transphobes, which of course will mean you have an overall more positive experience of the dating process. And the more pleasant the dating process is, the more likely it is to be a sustainable one, rather than one that requires a mental toughness and quickly becomes exhausting. Dating burnout can happen to anyone, but it is worth considering what will allow you an experience you can continue long enough to see benefits. There is no perfect option when it comes to disclosure, but it is worth considering what your needs and wants are from dating and if the strategies you are utilizing are allowing you to really access the results you would like.

CHAPTER 21

The Vulnerability of Sex

Sometimes the act of having sex or having sexual fantasies can be a person's catalyst for realizing they might not be cis. Sex is an extremely physically vulnerable act, and being nude or partially nude can activate all kinds of dysphoria. Genital dysphoria is the most obvious example, but even the act of taking off your shirt or not being able to edit the curves of your body with clothing can feel anxiety producing. Sex is also extremely emotionally vulnerable for many people, and it can also be one of the few places where adults indulge in fantasy. It is then no wonder that sex is one of the first places where things can start to feel off or where a sort of gender-related panic can make itself known.

A phrase you may have heard to help simplify sexuality and gender is that your sexuality is who you want to go to bed with, and your gender is who you want to go to bed as. Like all the other pithy phrases, it is far from perfect, but it does point out that your sexuality is not the only thing necessary to figure out in order to have pleasant romantic and sexual relationships. A lot of trans people initially come out as some form of queer before realizing that they are trans and then experience a second round of discovery around their sexuality. The second round must take the new information around gender identity into account, and even when the conclusion looks the same from the outside, the experience of coming out as a bisexual man vs a bisexual woman, for example, could feel brand new.

This is a lot of processing and self-discovery, and it takes time. For someone who identifies as a butch lesbian trans woman, or someone who identifies as a feminine bisexual trans masculine person, there is going to be a lot of stages to those discoveries. It is almost impossible to figure that out all at once and it could take multiple rounds of self-discovery to feel aligned personally and relationally. Gender and sexuality exist in relationship to one another, and some discoveries will be reliant on others in order to become clear.

With safe partners, sex can be a place to explore roles, dynamics, and acts that can provide information that will contribute to the larger picture of your gender identity.

Mitigating dysphoria during sex

While the vulnerability of sex can bring lots of new information, it can also bring its own complications, one of course being dysphoria. Sex can be a time when trans people feel their bodies are most exposed and focused on. Some strategies for mitigating dysphoria are physical and some are mental.

The most obvious way to prevent that is to limit bodily exposure, which could be anything from keeping clothes on, to keeping lights off, to staying under the covers. These strategies may work well enough, but sometimes they can feel like band-aid solutions to the issue and can be frustrating for all parties involved. What might feel good enough for a while can begin to feel insufficient, especially if one hopes to keep having sex and exploring all the different and exciting ways of having sex with a partner they would like to feel comfortable around. Feeling limited to having sex in the dark under the covers with their shirt on is not necessarily ideal for exploration.

With trustworthy partners it may feel more possible to try other ways of mitigating discomfort and dysphoria, and if they are not physical, then there are some mental strategies. It is common for trans people to need different language for different body parts. For example, substituting words like breasts for chest, or cock for clit, or vice versa. Even these small shifts can reduce dysphoria significantly, but sometimes people feel as if they are "playing pretend" or engaging in fantasy by using new language. I disagree, and I think whatever you call your body parts is what they are.

If you were to tell a cis man that his penis was too small so you have decided to not call it a penis, then you would be an asshole.[50] The same is true for using language with a trans masculine person. If you told a cis woman that her breasts were too small to be considered breasts, you would be the asshole. The same is true for a trans feminine person.

First, the sex you have is between you and your partners. The dynamics you have and the language you use only needs to work for those involved. This is not an experience where the world gets to weigh in on what you are doing. Second, it is crucial for your mental health that anyone you choose to be that vulnerable with is someone who respects you and understands the way you view and understand yourself. If what is between your legs is a clit to you, then it needs to be a clit for them as well. This is not an issue of them agreeing to a fantasy or delusion, this is about them respecting your identity and bodily autonomy. A relationship, even a casual sexual one, where your body is merely tolerated or used without the bare minimum of respect for your baseline needs is not only unsustainable but will start to eat at your mental health.

It is likely that with each new sexual partner, there will need to be at least some sort of discussion of the language you use for your body, the boundaries you have (what body parts can be touched or not touched, what body parts can be mentioned or not mentioned, etc.), and the sexual roles and actions you are interested in and available for. These conversations will also be necessary even if you have been in a long-term relationship and your understanding of your self is changing. In an ideal world, everyone would be having these discussions with new partners and checking in at regular intervals in any form of relationship, but most people are not taught enough about sex or boundaries to articulate their needs and wants. This can put the onus on trans people to initiate conversations like this.

It can feel like an awkward and complicated discussion to initiate, and there will be times when other people do not respond well to it. Sometimes that is out of their own discomfort of not knowing how to have this type of conversation, and sometimes it is because they are not interested in respecting your boundaries for whatever reason. Regardless of the reason, someone else's discomfort (or even annoyance/anger) is not a signal that you should ask less of partners. If a current or potential partner is able to work through their own discomfort to have this conversation and respect your needs, then that is great, but if they cannot, then that is information worth knowing, even if it hurts to hear. A negative reaction is not a signal that you are asking too much or being too much of a burden; it is a signal that for whatever reason, this person is not available to show up for you the way that you need them to. Your job in that scenario is not to beg for the respect that you deserve but to acknowledge that they have given you the information that they are not the person who will give you what you want and need.

Sexual baggage

Sex is stigmatized in much of society, and even for cis people this can mean sexual shame and baggage that is hard to shake. Many people receive the majority of their sexual education from pornography and other online information. This can be a much-needed resource, but it can also be a place where sexual hang-ups become obvious. The expansive backdrop of millions of sexual fantasies reveals internalized shame and questions about identity.

For some trans feminine people, watching feminization/sissification porn can be one of the first signals that they have questions around their gender. That genre of porn is also built on a premise of humiliation, and the combined effect of a humiliation-based fetish and the kinds of shame that can just exist from the narratives around "abandoning masculinity/maleness" makes it extremely hard to navigate without deeply complicated feelings. Many people are left to wonder if this interest is just a fetish or if it is actually about their gender identity. Combine that confusion with the many theories that that there are "real trans people" and people who simply have a fetish and play dress up, and you are going to have a mess that feels too shameful to even ask anyone about.

Autogynephilia was a term to describe "a male's propensity to be sexually aroused by the thought of himself as a female."[51] The theory of autogynephilia was described in the 1980s and '90s by sexologist Ray Blanchard as part of a taxonomy to distinguish different kinds of transvestites and transsexuals, based off the idea that there was a sexual reason for the so-called "cross-dressing" that explained why certain people were drawn to a feminine presentation.

The theory not-so-subtly undermines the validity of certain kinds of trans people's gender identities. One major critique of autogynephilia is that when you use the same sorts of scales to measure that same sexual arousal in cisgender women, they also qualify for the label. Or in other words, if you ask cis women if they are also sexually aroused by their own bodies and presenting in feminine ways, they will often answer yes.[52] The trans community on the whole has entirely dismissed this theory and finds it wildly insulting and not based on any scientific evidence.

This is another example of cisgender theorists making claims about the trans experience without the input of trans people and without even considering the greater implications of what they are saying. Blanchard claimed that autogynephilia does not exist in women (by which he meant cisgender women), and all the evidence has laughed in his face. Despite that, the legacy of autogynephilia has lived on and has continued to harm trans people in direct and indirect ways. It is rare to find a trans feminine person who has not had to contend with these types of ideas. They are an extremely common barrier that society has placed before trans feminine people in order to prove themselves as truly having a gendered experience rather than a sexually stigmatized experience.

Misgendering kinks and feminization

Sexual fantasies around feminization or misgendering are also far more common than people seem to believe, and many worry this invalidates their trans identity. As I mentioned, feminization/sissification kinks can be hard to parse, but they are often an early stage in determining that there is any kind of non-cis feeling around gender in the first place. This is not always a sexual thought and can show up simply as, *What if someone made me dress femininely or take hormones?* In fact, for the people who do indulge in it as a sexual fantasy, that may have more to do with the fact that these kinds of plot lines only exist in porn. Whether the original thought was tied to a sexual fantasy or not, people will often find the only spaces to explore the idea is in porn or erotica and it then becomes sexualized. This feeds the concern that it is only a fetish and not an aspect of their gender identity. Actually what is happening is that reading erotica or watching porn is the only time that some people allow themselves to think about a desire to be more feminine. To think about it outside of the bedroom potentially feels terrifying in a different way, which means that keeping it in the realm of a fetish is both worrying and comforting at the same time. It allows people to indulge in what might be a secret, shameful, or confused desire to present more femininely but at a time when they are not ready to acknowledge that this could be more meaningful than just as a sexual fantasy.

These kinds of gender-related thoughts are not just something that occurs for trans feminine people; nonbinary and trans masculine people can experience them too. Some trans masculine people will find that they are drawn to fantasies around being feminized as well. This usually happens on a different timeline than for trans feminine people and for an entirely different reason. For the trans masculine people who experience these fantasies, they can take place in the midst of social or physical transition.

Research has shown that for some people who have experienced (sexual) trauma, BDSM can be liberating and healing. This has a lot to do with the fact that within BDSM or other kink scenes there is a protective structure in place that is intended to keep all parties safe. Healthy BDSM involves negotiation, consent, and some kind of safe word or signal if things become too much for any reason. Unfortunately, this is very different from how most of us move through the rest of the world. We do not usually have a safe word to stop triggering conversations or have thorough negotiation before experiencing new activities with family or friends. Without those protective measures we can be much more easily harmed or triggered, even if it is accidental.

As a trans person, being misgendered is the primary experience until coming out, at which point it begins to lessen. For many years people use all kinds of words to refer to you without your consent, and sometimes you do not even realize you would like other ones. Either way, the effect of it builds up. Potentially you have 15, 25, 35, 45, or more years of being misgendered built up. Then what happens when you finally have the ability to control what is happening to you and what words people use to refer to you and your body? You might have some trauma you would like to process in a safe environment. For some trans masculine and nonbinary people this can feel like the first time that they have control over how their body is feminized. In this context it takes place with their consent, rather than without it, and in a scene that has been negotiated in advance and with the ability to shut it down at a moment's notice. This can be a powerful experience when the majority of your past gendered experiences have felt out of your hands.

For many people, the vulnerability of sex is what makes these such powerful experiences and allows people to bypass some of their mental defenses in order to access important information. The vulnerability skips past intellectualization and is instead a bodily and emotional experience. While these kinks do exist for different reasons for different people depending on their gender history, they certainly do not invalidate anyone's gender identity. For some, they are a way to begin to access their gender identity, and for others they are a way to process past gender-related harm or trauma. There is no need for them to be meaningful or healing in order to be legitimate expressions of sexuality, but whether they are or not, these thoughts and fantasies do not have meaning to a person's gender identity unless they feel meaningful to that individual. There is no clinician in the world who can take these sexual experiences and use them to diagnose or determine someone's gender identity. You are the only person who has the power and ability to determine what they mean for you.

Do hormones make you gay?

Depending on what parts of the internet you have searched for answers, you might have come across concerned threads about if hormones change a person's sexuality. Or frequently the question is just worded as, "Do hormones make you gay?" The short answer is no, hormones do not make you gay. The long answer is that hormones can allow people to have a more expansive experience of their sexuality and sometimes this includes an attraction to more genders than they initially thought they were attracted to.

For some trans people who were particularly shut off from their sexuality before physical transition, this can be a more jarring process. Occasionally that does mean that people who thought they were solely attracted to women find out they are solely attracted to men and vice versa, but it is not common. What is much more likely to happen is that people who thought they were solely attracted to men find out that they are also attracted to some women, and some nonbinary people too. Perhaps after the process of exploring their own gender they realize they barely understand what gender even is in a larger sense and find they do not know how to define the genders of people they are attracted to when they can barely describe gender at all. Perhaps they just know what they are into when they see it and maybe they are actually just attracted to a certain kind of masculine energy, but it remains to be seen and more data is needed. Perhaps all of the above. As we have seen, gender and sexuality have a relational experience, which means there are infinite ways that sexuality could present as you become more comfortable with yourself.

Many trans people find that who they were attracted to pre-transition was partially their sexuality, but it was also partially an attempt to feel a certain way around their partners. If they desired to feel more masculine, they may have been drawn to partners who were more feminine so they could feel like the more masculine person in comparison. And if they desired to feel more feminine, they may have sought out more masculine partners in order to feel like the more feminine person in the partnership. Many find that being on hormones can start to mean that they could still feel feminine around feminine people or that they could still feel masculine around masculine people. They no longer feel as limited in choosing a partner based on how that partner's gender expression feels in relation to their own.

Hormones can also change the way people experience their sex drive or sexuality. Obviously testosterone can increase someone's sex drive and a testosterone blocker (like spironolactone) can reduce it. But sexuality is not just a single scale with a high sex drive on one end and a low sex drive on the other. Even sex drive and sexual arousal are not a single, binary on/off switch, and they are affected by many factors.

It is hard to understand any of these factors in a vacuum because hormone dosages are never the single variable that is changing. While on hormones you continue to live your life, and then there are the cyclical experiences whereby hormones change the way people experience and respond to you, which can change the way you experience and respond to people, which can change the way people experience and respond to you, and so on for a while. This also occurs on an internal level. If the version of yourself that you see in the mirror changes, then that can affect the way you experience yourself, and that can change your interest or desire in sexual relationships.

Sexual changes are unlikely to be solely due to hormones, ormones can be a piece of or a catalyst for those changes. ty is complex enough to try to understand without all ing pieces, but hormonal transition is a time when so many physical, emotional, and relational pieces are shifting at once that it is impossible to identify a singular cause.

Trans people frequently notice a sexual shift during hormonal transition, but what that shift looks like depends on the person. It can be anything from a changing desire to be dominant or submissive, top or bottom, or even changing desire around roles, fantasies, and actions. Again, often change means expansion rather than deciding you hate what you used to love.

This can appear overwhelming or scary. Many trans people are afraid to lose things that they have enjoyed or may have structured parts of their identity around. It is an understandable fear, but it is rare that people feel like they are losing aspects of themselves or their sexuality. It is far more common to feel they gain understanding about more facets of their sexuality. The things that fall away often feel as if they needed to fall away because they no longer serve them in their more authentic gender identity and expression.

CHAPTER 22

How to Deal with the People Who Make Your Gender a Big Deal

Regardless of how comfortable you become in your own gender identity, there will be people around you who do not understand, do not know how to support you, or even sadder still, do not want to support you. It is important to keep in mind that other people in your life are going to be significantly behind at processing this news. By the time you have the confidence to let someone know your gender identity, you have most likely been thinking about it for months, if not years. You could be on day 800 of consciously coming to terms with your gender identity, and then you inform your mom, who is now at day one. This is a significant gap. They will also need time to integrate the new information the same way you did. You likely also initially responded to your trans identity with denial, confusion, or anger, and it took time to understand and accept it for yourself.

Dealing with someone else's shock can be confusing and upsetting when it feels like your gender identity should have been somewhat obvious. Maybe you were the kid who was wearing your sister's dresses every day after school or maybe you were the kid who peed standing up until an adult told you that you were not allowed to do that. In some way, you may have been fighting against your assumed gender role and presentation for decades. Then your parents or caregivers who witnessed all of that claim they never saw this trans thing coming. Maybe that was not your experience, but instead you have been subtly trying to drop hints for years and they have not picked up on a single one.

Either way, it is okay to feel your feelings around that disconnect. You may feel disappointment or anger. You may be confused or incredulous. Feel whatever you are feeling and allow other people to have their own experience as well. That does not mean that you have to agree with their experience or you have to endorse it, simply that you allow them to have it. Maybe that means they need to look at the past through a new lens before they are able to integrate the news. People see what they want to see, so for many parents they are too close to you as their child to see what may be obvious to everyone else.

Every parent has expectations for their child. Sometimes those are extremely specific: They want their child to be a doctor, to get married to a white-collar professional, to have at least three children, and to live down the block so they can babysit their grandkids. Sometimes parents make claims that they do not have expectations for their child until something unexpected happens and they realize this was not how they pictured things playing out. You will hear some parents say they do not care what their child grows up to be, they just want them to be "happy and healthy." But the assumption of gender (and sexuality) can be very foundational. If your parent believes they will be fine if you grow up to be an artist, doctor, salesperson, chef, plumber, or teacher, but it never crosses their mind that maybe you are not a girl, then that will be jarring, because they tried to prepare themselves for an incomplete set of possibilities.

It is never possible to prepare yourself for all possibilities. This is a nice fantasy that is intended to protect yourself from the unexpected, but it is just a fantasy. In a world where it has not crossed your parents' minds that your gender could be different than their expectation, they will inevitably see you through that lens even when all signs might point to it being inaccurate. You might come out to your aunts or uncles, your cousins, your siblings, your step-parents, and their reactions might be far less shocked. You might even get reactions like, "Oh yeah, that makes sense" or, "I always kind of knew." That's because they had a different experience of you growing up that did not include the same kinds of hopes, dreams, expectations, and fantasies that your parents might have had. Ironically, those more distant family or community members were able to see you more clearly than the people you might have spent the most time with.

It can be hard to feel hopeful around certain people's reactions. Sometimes they will say very hurtful things when you are in this process of extreme vulnerability. They could tell you that you are wrong, that they do not believe you, that you are misunderstanding yourself, that you have been influenced by other trans people into thinking you are trans, or any number of dismissive things. Do your best not to suppress your hurt, but also allow this to be their initial reaction rather than their final reaction. Just as you needed time to process your own gender, so will they. Generally, except in the cases where someone entirely cuts you off or disowns you, whatever their initial response is will grow to be more accepting in time. It may never look how you hoped it would and it may not be in the timeline you had hoped for, but if there is a tiny kernel of openness or willingness to hear your experience, it will expand. It is up to you to determine if what they have to offer is what you are willing to accept, and it is up to you to determine if you want to or have the ability to give them time.

Giving someone time does not look like holding their hand through this process or giving them an audience to air every single grievance or thought they have along the way. Sometimes the healthiest thing for you to do for yourself is to stay far away from them during this time while they process. Sometimes a necessary boundary is having no contact. This is going to be based on your specific relationship to determine what is best for you. No matter what your specific relationship is like, you will need to determine the boundaries of what you are available for and what you feel comfortable with. For example, if your dad keeps calling you to repeat something he read on a transphobic religious website, you are not required to listen to it, and you do not have to debate him, and you do not have to grit your teeth and white-knuckle your way through the call until he is done. You can tell him that you are uninterested in discussing that and that if he continues to talk about it, then you will hang up the phone.

This is not easy to do, but it is freeing. Setting boundaries is one of the hardest things to learn how to do, and it is extremely hard with close family members. But it is critical that if you set a boundary, you follow through with maintaining it if your boundary is crossed. If you tell someone that if they keep discussing something, you will hang up the phone, then you have to hang up the phone if they keep discussing it. What happens if you do not is they learn that your boundaries are suggestions and they do not need to be taken seriously. They have learned that they can push them and push them until they might as well not exist at all. They learn that this is a game.

A boundary is not a demand or an ultimatum. A boundary does not say, *You have to* or, *You cannot*, because other people's actions are not within our control. A good boundary says, *You can do whatever you would like to do, and here is how I will respond.* In other words, you can do whatever you want to do and I can do whatever I want to do. A good boundary is clear and it has a clear outcome if crossed.

Having boundaries can also make other people very mad. Sometimes people feel entitled to your time, your energy, your explanations, and your patience. The certainty with which they believe that does not make it true. And the first time you enforce a boundary with someone, it could feel disastrous. You could do everything "right" and then after you hang up on your dad he calls you six times in a row where you do not pick up and he leaves increasingly angry voicemails. It is very hard to feel like you did the right thing in that circumstance. You will doubt your actions and wonder if you are being selfish or dramatic. It is certainly a discouraging way to start maintaining boundaries.

It is important to remember that you were clear with them and that you simply followed through with what you said. This was not a surprise to them, and they made a choice to continue the action they knew would result in an action from you.

People will imply, or maybe even outright say, that your coming out was something that you did to them. This is another thing we internalize. We believe that by being trans and "making people deal with it" we are imposing on other people. The only reason we believe this is because everyone is assumed to be cis until proven otherwise, so you have to take an action of "coming out" or informing people that their assumptions about you were incorrect. It feels like an imposition because it could require all these new actions from others. People might now have to call you a new name, or by new pronouns, and think of you different-ly. But imagine you are a cis person and you introduce yourself as Micah to a new coworker, and then you find out weeks later that they have been calling you Michael. Sure, correcting them weeks later could be incredibly awkward, but you hopefully would not stop to think, *Well, they think my name is Michael, so I cannot ever tell them they have been wrong. I guess I have to change my name to Michael now.* Correcting someone's misunderstanding or assumption is not an imposition.

By beginning to believe that you are not imposing on other people, it is much easier to maintain boundaries. Just because someone made a false assumption about your identity does not mean that you are obligated to play along with it.

Correcting people

It is easy to get overwhelmed at the prospect of correcting when people misgender you. First, it is important to take it one step at a time. Before it happens, do not get ahead of yourself and imagine how many times you might have to correct people. Take each instance as it comes and try your best not to anticipate it and the feelings of anxiety that can come with it. Remember what we discussed about anxiety and how to continue to bring yourself back to the present. Second, know that you are not obligated to be perfect at this, and it is not possible to be.

Sometimes you will be comfortable enough to correct people in the moment and sometimes you will feel overwhelmed and exhausted and unable to say a single word. That is normal. There are countless factors that are going to contribute to whether or not you feel able to correct someone and a lot of it will boil down to how safe the setting feels. If you are interacting with strangers, or in a strange setting, or around people you know to hold transphobic views, then of course it will feel much more difficult to correct someone. And the honest truth is that sometimes it is not even safe to do this in some settings. But factors like how tired you are, and if you have had a hard day, and if you will ever see these people again and therefore does it feel important to correct them, will also affect whether it feels possible or important to correct people. Your brain and body could be crunching those numbers behind the scenes and you are not even going to be fully aware of what is contributing to your ability to say something or not. (That constant mental math is also exhausting so when your mind tells you that you have no reason to feel so tired, I assure you that you do. Allow yourself gentleness and rest here too.)

This is how it played out in my own life in early transition: I would be out in the world and someone would misgender me. First, I would experience the bodily sensation that felt close to getting slapped in the face or punched in the stomach. I would feel like I was reeling. Then my brain would start up and would start asking why this happened. *Was it the way I was walking? Was it my clothes? Was it my height? Was it that they realized it was unlikely I was a 15-year-old boy hanging out with*

20- to 30-year-olds and therefore I must be a woman? Then I would start trying to problem solve and see if this was something I could do something about or prevent in the future. Then finally my brain would ask myself if I should correct them.

Sometimes this happened in a split second and sometimes I fully dissociated while my brain did this for minutes. By that time the conversation could have progressed three topics, or sometimes the person who had misgendered me had already walked away. In the circumstances where this was with a stranger that I was not going to interact with again, it was easier to let go (not easy, just easier), but with people who I was going to continue to have some interactions with in the future I would beat myself up for not taking the opportunity to correct them or stand up for myself.

In actuality, there is not always a whole lot you can do to bypass that internal mental process. Sometimes your mind just has to run through it, and it is important to be kind to yourself after the fact. You did not fail to stand up for yourself. You just dealt with something uncomfortable or painful and you experienced that hurt.

After that you still have a few options. One that seems somewhat obvious, but often is not, is that you can correct someone later. You can text them hours or even days later and say, "Hey, I noticed you misgendered me earlier. I didn't say anything in the moment but just so you know my pronouns are she/her or they/them." You can say more if you want to, but you also do not have any obligation to explain what was going on for you internally and how you felt about it. Another option is utilizing the people in your life who want to be allies but do not know how to support you. You will have some friends and coworkers and other people in your life who want to be as supportive as possible and tell you to let them know if there is anything they can do to help. It can be hard to find something they can help with but here is one practical task: Tell them to correct people on your behalf. Be specific and tell them how you would like them to say it and in what settings. You can tell them to be as specific as to say, "Actually he uses he/him pronouns" or you can tell them, "If someone is talking about me using she pronouns, can you make sure to say some sentences where you refer to me by he/him pronouns in front of them so they hear it?" Make sure they also know if there are times or settings where you do not want them to do this for you. Otherwise let them loose and let them carry some of this burden for you.

Somewhere along the way, many people start to believe that they have to come up with a firm stance about whether they are going to be a good trans educator or if they are going to be the kind of person who tells people to google it every time something comes up. Or in other words, are you going to be the person who is patient and explains things 100 percent of the time or the person who explains things 0 percent of the time? You do not have to be either. In fact, I would suggest you do not be either. No matter how comfortable you are in your gender identity and how much of an extrovert you might be, there will be times when you are tired and there will be times when someone on the bus or someone in a comment thread online will demand you give them a thorough explanation. You do not owe everyone this, but you may choose to give it in certain relationships and in certain settings because it feels worthwhile. On the other hand, if you come out to your partner of five years and they start asking questions about you and your gender and you tell them to leave you alone and to google all of it, well, that might not go well for either of you. Even with the people you love and care about the most, you may not be available to answer every question, but there is no resource online or in print that is going to give your loved ones answers about you specifically. It is important to assess yourself and the relationship to determine what is appropriate and comfortable.

Each time someone asks you to explain, it is important to check in with yourself. Check if you feel safe in this setting and with these people and that you do not feel overly tired—physically or emotionally. Check if that question feels like something that is important for you to answer or if you just feel obligated to answer. Check if that question feels like it needs your input specifically or if perhaps there is a resource that this person could read or watch or listen to that could help them understand.

Many trans people feel as if they have to make sure their friends and family keep up. They feel an obligation to make sure that people know that their trans identity is real and that all trans identities are real. They feel obligated to educate everyone on the biology and the psychology and the sociology of it. Whether you do that or not, people will show up or they will not. You cannot curate a perfect set of articles, and graphs, and verses, and documentaries to make someone listen if they are not open to it. You cannot drag people along behind you. As you walk along your own path, do not keep looking back and checking to see who is following you. You will know who is with you on this journey, and if other people are straggling behind and eventually catch up, you will know when they are finally there by your side. And for those who never seem to take any steps at all, do not keep looking back begging them to follow you. They will show up or they will not. It may not be at the speed you would like, and unfortunately sometimes it may not be at all, but you do not have to do anything but determine what you need for yourself and give yourself the space to grieve if you need to.

When someone apologizes for misgendering you, it is important not to respond by saying that it is fine if it does not feel fine. This can be a hard habit to break, and for many people that "It's fine" answer has become almost a tic. We have certain scripts in our minds for common social interactions, and like saying, "I'm good" when asked how you are (even if you definitely are not good), sometimes we respond before even thinking about the answer. The script many of us have learned in apologies is to say it is fine or it is no big deal. Unfortunately, when you tell people something is fine, then they might believe that it is indeed fine. It is shocking, I know. If instead you respond by saying, "Thank you for the apology," then the other person is far more likely to integrate that as something they need to continue to try doing better at. Whereas by being told it is fine, they might also let themselves off the hook from keeping trying. We do not mean to sabotage the progress, but it can be hard to not feel guilty when someone is apologizing and taking accountability for their mistake. It may continue to feel awkward to respond to apologies in a new way, but do not sabotage their progress and your own comfort if you do not have to.

When trying becomes too painful

There are times when none of this will work and even continually trying to maintain boundaries in a relationship is too overwhelming and too painful. There is no minimum or maximum amount of effort you are required to put in before you are allowed to make a decision to cut someone out of your life. Sometimes these severed ties need to be permanent, but they can also be what needs to happen temporarily. No matter how much you try, there will be people who believe you did not do enough to maintain the relationship. There is a commonly held belief that family is family and you are obligated to keep them around even when they harm you. That is not the case, and you are not obligated to keep interacting with someone who harms you. But how do you respond when your aunt calls you and begs you to come to the New Year's celebration and does not understand why you cannot just deal with your mom for a few hours? Maybe you manage to hold firm, and then your grandfather calls you and tells you to stop being selfish and whatever is going on between you and your mom is not that serious, and it is not more important than being with your family. Each time your boundaries are pushed, the more you will doubt yourself. But you are the only person who gets to determine when something is causing more harm than happiness and when a dynamic is not tolerable anymore.

As we already discussed, having boundaries can make people upset and angry, but boundaries can also disrupt the status quo of a whole family or community. We might not realize it, but every family has unspoken rules and roles. No one sits you down at five years old and explains those rules to you, but somehow you might still learn, for example, that you should not get in the middle of a fight between your mom and dad, and that if your dad is in the garage it means you shouldn't talk to him, and that you and all your siblings know your sister sneaks out sometimes and no one says anything. Maybe you have taken on the role of the straight-A student, or the star athlete, or the jokester, or the fuck up. No one has a family meeting and decides who gets which role, but all the roles serve a purpose in keeping the whole (maybe wildly dysfunctional) machine chugging along and everyone knows they have to do their part. It functions in its dysfunction.

Something as big as a gender transition can upend the whole structure. Sometimes that happens because it means you are playing a different role than the one you were assigned, but sometimes it means you have had enough revelations about your life and mental health that you are setting boundaries for the first time and no one in your family has ever done that before. Maybe it is both. Either way, everyone may now see you as the one who changed everything, and how dare you! This is particularly frustrating when you can see everyone suffering under the rules and roles, and it feels like the change should be welcomed. But change is scary and it is rarely welcomed. Perhaps everyone hates their role but at least they know how to play it. They wonder if they can play a different one that they have never practiced. A change requires an initial conflict, and it involves learning new information. They are mad at you for making them do all that work.

One of my professors described a family as a group of people standing on a platform that is balanced on a ball. If one person takes a step forward, then everyone else has to adjust in order to keep the platform from falling. Each time someone shifts, everyone else must react in order to keep it stable. It is exhausting but it feels like it is what you have to do. After all, you can't just let everyone fall. Then, if someone decides that they do not want to be stuck in this pattern for their mental health or safety, they are stepping off the platform entirely. This means everyone else must react dramatically. This is the most precarious point, and everyone else may feel as if that person made them unnecessarily fight for the balance again. Of course, everyone else can step off the platform too, but they may have not realized that yet. They may see the person stepping off as an act of madness or wild rebellion, rather than a way for that person who stepped off to care for themselves.

It can feel crucial to decide who to keep trying with and who to cut out immediately. It can seem like there is a pressure to know if you will continue to engage and to know if you cut someone off if it will be temporary or permanent. It is not necessary to know right away, nor may it be possible to know right away. You can make a decision day by day and minute by minute. Allow yourself to determine what is good for you right now, and tomorrow allow yourself to decide what is good for you tomorrow. That can be as big or as small as it needs to be. That could look like deciding whether to answer a phone call from your dad as it happens, instead of deciding, *Will I always pick up his calls or will I never pick up his calls?* Instead, it may mean pausing when he calls and asking yourself if you have the ability and energy to speak to him in that moment.

Perhaps you notice a pattern of not wanting to engage consistently and it becomes permanent, or perhaps it is consistent for a few months until the circumstances change enough. Either way, you will find out as it unfolds, knowing that you are doing what is right for you.

CHAPTER 23

Becoming a Representative for the Trans Community

When you come out as trans, you may be awarded the title of Official Unofficial Representative of the Trans Community. This is an interesting position because it's not one that you even have to apply for before it is awarded to you. You wake up one day and suddenly feel burdened with the duties that this role entails. Being a representative asks that you speak on behalf of the entire trans community, give answers for what all trans people like or do not like and want or do not want, and that your actions can be representative for all trans people. It also asks you to not do anything embarrassing, because everyone is watching. You are a diplomat from the country of Trans to the country of Cis. And, of course, it is an unpaid position.

This is unfortunately pretty common when you are a member of a statistically small community. Or even if you are just a statistically small community compared with the person you are interacting with (e.g. the guy who says, "You're the only Chinese person I know." China actually has over a billion people and therefore being Chinese is statistically common, just not statistically common to that guy).

Despite most of us knowing that this is an unreasonable expectation to have for a single person, we internalize it anyway. It is easier to fight against that demand to speak for the entire community than it is to shake the feeling that you could embarrass the whole community, or that you could do it wrong. Further, we start to fear that other trans people might also think we are doing it wrong and that we are embarrassing every trans person. The pressure comes from both sides. What if trans *and* cis people think you are a terrible trans person?

Well it is extremely unlikely, but the pressure from the cis community generally has a lot more to do with cis people not wanting to do the work to understand more than one person's experience. They ask you to be a representative for the community so they can get a quick and easy answer that does not require reading books or listening to the experiences of more than one trans person. Sometimes it is because they want someone to cosign their bad behavior. Maybe someone told them to not say "tranny" and they believe if they can find one trans person who is fine with the word, then they can be absolved of their sins. If they can do that, then they do not have to change, and they can believe the person who asked them to stop is being overdramatic or too sensitive. You are not responsible for any of that mess. You do not have to educate anyone, and you certainly do not have to perform any emotional response for someone else's comfort. If an ally needs you to cosign their behavior or be calm when you tell them not to use harmful language, then they are not an ally. With allies like these, who needs enemies? A true ally will sit down, shut up, and gather enough information to find out what could actually be useful to the community, rather than what they think could be useful.

On the other side, the feeling that the trans community might think you are doing your transness wrong usually has a lot more to do with a feeling of impostor syndrome. You may still be struggling to convince yourself that your feelings are valid or that you are actually allowed to call yourself trans. That is normal, and in fact it is the most relatable trans experience out there. We are back to the initial question of, "Am I trans enough? Am I trans enough for myself and am I trans enough for the community?" The community does not see your self-doubt the way that you do. Some may be too wrapped up in their own feelings of self-doubt to notice, or they may have an incredible amount of empathy for that feeling of not being enough. The other members of the trans community who can see your doubt know exactly what that feels like.

Unfortunately, there are trans people who have been so traumatized by their experiences that they inflict it on others. There are people who believe that because they had a hard time accessing care, you should also have to jump through the hoops that they were required to jump through. They believe that being harassed or judged is something that you just have to learn to accept. This is not just a belief system that exists around trans trauma. A truly American example is those who believe that it would be unfair to forgive student loan debt because they had to pay theirs off for decades, or that universal healthcare is unfair because they had to pay for their healthcare. They believe it would be unfair to them if other people have it easier. Instead of pointing their anger at the source of it, they point it toward those they see as receiving an unearned benefit. But we all deserve to understand ourselves, feel comfortable in our bodies and our communities, and have access to the care that would provide that.

I would argue that the only way to be a bad member of the trans community is to be cruel to trans people, and that includes yourself. You are both trans enough for yourself and you are trans enough for the trans community. There will always be people who challenge that, whether that is out of their own discomfort and lack of knowledge or because of their own trauma and internalized narratives around trans identity. Your trans identity is not up for public debate. And once your trans identity is not up for your own personal debate, it is easier to exist in that truth. Once you arrive at a place where you are confident that your identity is yours and yours alone, it becomes ridiculous when someone challenges it. You will be able to laugh and move on. You will be too busy living your best trans life.

CHAPTER 24

A Hopeful End

W hether you started this book questioning your gender, already knowing that you are trans, or even as
a curious ally, you have explored some new places
within yourself.

There have been some heavy moments throughout, and I
hope you have been able to care for yourself while reading it.
If you have struggled to give yourself space for self-care, or if
you did a speed run through these pages, then please take the
time to check in with what you need now. Check in with your
mind but also check in with your gut. All parts of you are giving you signals now about your needs and about the fears and
insecurities that need caretaking. Breathe deeply. Don't panic.
Care for your most terrified self with your most gentle self. Take
a walk, call a friend, listen to some music, hug your pet, drink
some water. And once you feel safe and secure in your body,
then take a moment to celebrate this accomplishment. (I can
feel some of you rolling your eyes from where I sit. I know you're
thinking *therapists are really corny.* This is the last corny thing
I'll ask of you.) You were open to exploring your own identity
and challenging what you know, and that is worth celebrating.

As I progressed through my own process of discovering my gender identity, I eventually reached a breaking point where I knew I had to think less and do more. Thinking brought me to an impenetrable wall that not even my imagination could see past. I longed for some sort of X-ray vision to be able to see through the wall and into my future, and it never came. We have the fantasy that just one more book or video or conversation will be the assurance we need to make the perfect decision. Even though you know the doubt is normal, maybe you will be the one who does not have to make mistakes or change directions along the path. Maybe if you just sit on these concerns a little while longer, it will all come together fully formed. But the only way to find out who you are becoming is to undergo the process to become.

You have no obligation to decide what you are going to do right now. This process gets to be as big or as small or as fast or as slow as you would like it to be. If it feels too overwhelming to figure out what happens next, then allow yourself to not figure that out right now. It is fine if you just read some words and that is it. Perhaps those words will be a seed that was planted and they will sprout with time. Perhaps they are just ideas. Take what you like and leave the rest.

Being trans can be an incredibly joyful experience and there can be many hurdles that can make it hard to reach that joy, but you deserve to experience it. You deserve to live long enough to see it. You deserve the best version of your life. You deserve your truth. You deserve a life that has not been unnecessarily limited by other people. Let yourself feel what it means to deserve your joy. And if you can't hold that right now, then let me hold it for you until it feels possible for you to hold. You deserve all the joy and happiness that your authentic life will bring you.

Thanks for being here on this earth having an intentional experience of your gender and yourself. There is no way to do it wrong. You have already started, and you are doing great.

More Resources

GENERAL

Everything You Ever Wanted to Know about Trans (But Were Afraid to Ask), Brynn Tannehill

How to Understand Your Gender: A Practical Guide for Exploring Who You Are, Alex Iantaffi and Meg-John Barker

Transgender History: The Roots of Today's Revolution, Susan Stryker

Yes, You Are Trans Enough: My Transition from Self-Loathing to Self-Love, Mia Violet

GENDER WORKBOOKS

The Trans Self-Care Workbook: A Coloring Book and Journal for Trans and Non-Binary People, Theo Lorenz

Trans Survival Workbook, Owl Fisher and Fox Fisher

Transition to Success: A Self-Esteem and Confidence Workbook for Trans People, Matthew Waites

My Gender Workbook: How to Become a Real Man, a Real Woman, the Real You, or Something Else Entirely, Kate Bornstein

You and Your Gender Identity: A Guide to Discovery, Dara Hoffman-Fox

MENTAL HEALTH

A Liberated Mind: How to Pivot Toward What Matters, Steven C. Hayes

Gender Trauma: Healing Cultural, Social, and Historical Gendered Trauma, Alex Iantaffi

Healing the Fragmented Selves of Trauma Survivors: Overcoming Internal Self-Alienation, Janina Fisher

No Bad Parts: Healing Trauma and Restoring Wholeness with the Internal Family Systems Model, Richard C. Schwartz

Retelling the Stories of Our Lives: Everyday Narrative Therapy to Draw Inspiration and Transform Experience, David Denborough

Set Boundaries, Find Peace: A Guide to Reclaiming Yourself, Nedra Glover Tawwab

The Anxiety Book for Trans People: How to Conquer Your Dysphoria, Worry Less and Find Joy, Freiya Benson

The Mindful Way through Depression: Freeing Yourself from Chronic Unhappiness, Mark Williams, John Teasdale, Zindel Segal and Jon Kabat-Zinn

The Trans Guide to Mental Health and Well-Being, Katy Lees

AUTISM

NeuroTribes: The Legacy of Autism and the Future of Neurodiversity, Steve Silberman

Spectrums: Autistic Transgender People in Their Own Words, Maxfield Sparrow (editor)

Supporting Transgender Autistic Youth and Adults: A Guide for Professionals and Families, Finn V. Gratton

The Autistic Trans Guide to Life, Yenn Purkis and Wenn B. Lawson

Trans and Autistic: Stories from Life at the Intersection, Noah Adams and Bridget Liang

SEX

Fucking Trans Women, Mira Bellwether

Trans Bodies, Trans Selves: A Resource by and for the Transgender Community, Laura Erickson-Schroth (editor)

Trans Sex: Clinical Approaches to Trans Sexualities and Erotic Embodiments, Lucie Fielding

THEORY

Gender Trouble, Judith Butler

Nobody Passes: Rejecting the Rules of Gender and Conformity, Mattilda a.k.a. Matt Bernstein Sycamore (editor)

Undoing Gender, Judith Butler

MEMOIRS

Heaven, Emerson Whitney

In Their Shoes: Navigating Non-Binary Life, Jamie Windust

I'm Afraid of Men, Vivek Shraya

Man Alive: A True Story of Violence, Forgiveness and Becoming a Man, Thomas Page McBee

Redefining Realness: My Path to Womanhood, Identity, Love & So Much More, Janet Mock

We Both Laughed in Pleasure: The Selected Diaries of Lou Sullivan 1961-1991, Ellis Martin and Zach Ozma (editors)

Whipping Girl: A Transsexual Woman on Sexism and the Scapegoating of Femininity, Julia Serano

Notes

1   Informed consent care gives trans people far more (although usually not exclusive) power to make decisions for themselves and decide if they would like to begin hormones without having to be deemed officially trans enough.

2   If you're interested in workbooks or other recommendations, see the More Resources section.

3   Did anyone else have this experience during quarantine? Grappling with a 1000-piece puzzle thinking it would be fun and then cursing your hubris? Just me? That's fine, I won't make you endure puzzle metaphors for the whole book.

4   It's called confirmation bias, and you may have heard it mentioned once or twice when it comes to the political climate or the state of large-scale attempts to address global health risks.

5   Brown, G.R. (1989) "Transsexuals in the military: flight into hypermasculinity." *Archives of Sexual Behavior*, 17, 6, 527–537.

6   Originally used in Brown, G.R. (1988) "Transsexuals in the military: flight into hypermasculinity." *Archives of sexual behavior* 17(6). doi: 10.1007/BF01542340

7   Where body positivity can be useful for trans people is when they have a body that feels aligned with their sense of self and being able to say, *I don't feel bad about my body, you all are making me feel bad about my body!* For example, a trans person who feels comfortable with having breasts and a penis, or a trans person who feels comfortable with having a flat chest and a vagina, or a trans person who wears makeup and has a beard: all of those people can then utilize body positivity to say that there is nothing wrong with their presentation and there should be space in our society to exist in these bodies without scorn or disapproval.

8   Please don't ask any further questions about this metaphor I did not have to include.

9   The terms "passing" and "passable" are not ones that everyone in the community identifies with, but they are defined as the experience of being consistently perceived as your gender. Frequently this can be a shortened form of "cis-passing," which means you can move through the world and be assumed to be cisgender. While some trans people don't aspire to that goal personally, others have taken on the belief that no trans people should want to be cis-passing. The desire to pass is primarily an issue of safety at its core, and perhaps this goes back to what was discussed in Chapter 5, The Paradox of Transition. Is this desire vain or does it have a social benefit that cannot be ignored? Many trans people don't live in a place where they can ignore the safety concerns of not passing long term.

10   For more specific information around fertility timelines, please speak to a trans-affirming medical provider early on in the process of medical transition. Sperm banking and egg retrieval exist to keep the possibility of fertility longer than it could exist otherwise.

11   "One problem with that view of social construction is that it suggests that what trans people feel about what their gender is, and should be, is itself 'constructed' and, therefore, not real. And then the feminist police comes along to expose the construction and dispute a trans person's sense of their lived reality. I oppose this use of social construction absolutely, and consider it to be a false, misleading, and oppressive use of the theory." From: The TERFs (May 1 2014) "Judith Butler addresses TERFs and the work of Sheila Jeffreys and Janice Raymond." https://theterfs.com/2014/05/01

12   More on this in Chapter 18, On Being a Trans Woman.

13   For more on social construction of gender specifically, see Judith Butler's *Gender Trouble* and *Undoing Gender*.

14   This is my own language; the actual text says "boys."

15   This is my own language; the actual text says "girls."

16   They cite incredibly large ranges of persistence rates and then say that they don't know if encouraging these children results in higher rates of persistence, because there hasn't been long-term research yet. At least not the kind of research that the DSM authors deem to be acceptable. It's a professional shrug of responsibility regarding if the diagnosis is any good at identifying trans children.

17   Dissociation is disconnecting from your thoughts, feelings, memories, or sense of self. It can range from a mild experience that many people call "zoning out" to something much more severe.

18 There are a lot of fears people have about medical transition based on myths or outdated information. It is important to make sure the medical information that you are accessing is from a reputable source and is the most up to date available. *Trans Bodies, Trans Selves: A Resource for the Transgender Community* (edited by Laura Erickson-Schroth) can be a good place to start. It includes a lot of information about transgender health, surgery, and hormones. It can also be extremely useful to speak to doctors who specialize in this work and get your specific medical questions answered.

19 Detransition is when someone returns to identifying as the sex they were assigned at birth. This can also come along with reversing social, medical, and legal changes that may have already been undergone as well.

20 Wiepjes, C.M. et al. (2018) "The Amsterdam Cohort of Gender Dysphoria Study (1972–2015): trends in prevalence, treatment, and regrets." *Journal of Sexual Medicine*, 15, 4, 582–590.

21 The removal of the testes or ovaries.

22 Intellectualizing is attempting to ignore or shut down emotions in order to be purely rational.

23 Also known as the Kübler-Ross theory.

24 If this is your experience, seeking out professional anger management support can offer new techniques to manage those feelings in non-destructive ways.

25 Dr. Dan Siegel [NICABM] (2019, August 2) "Why trauma affects some people more than others, with Dan Siegel" [Video]. Youtube. https://www.youtube.com/watch?v=yb4dgkkokEk

26 Other forms of dissociation like depersonalization (not feeling like a person or feeling outside of yourself) and derealization (feeling like the outside world is not real or is artificial in some way) can also occur.

27 Compartmentalization allows conflicting thoughts, feelings, ideas, or identities to coexist by keeping them separate.

28 I use the phrase "first adolescence" to discuss the physical, social, and emotional experiences that generally come alongside natal puberty. Whereas for trans people, a "second adolescence" includes some of the experiences that can come alongside physical and social transition.

29 Warrier, V., Greenberg, D.M., Weir, E. et al. (2020) "Elevated rates of autism, other neurodevelopmental and psychiatric diagnoses, and autistic traits in transgender and gender-diverse individuals." *Nature Communications*, 11, 3959.

30 A name for the way different brains are wired.

31 For the purposes of this section, I will speak more broadly about

neurodivergence rather than speaking to specific neurotypes. Because many of the traits of ASD and ADHD overlap, and because many people are reliant on self-diagnosis (for many reasons, including lack of access to resources and testing), it is difficult to pull those apart as separate experiences when relying on self-reporting. And in the case of this section, it may not be the most useful to do so. As you would suspect, aside from the data on prevalence rates, there is little research about how exactly neurodivergence and trans identities intersect. Research on how and why these types of overlaps occur can quickly turn to questions about how to prevent these traits from developing (i.e. eugenics), and many activists are rightfully wary of who is conducting that kind of research and what those researchers or others intend to do with the results. Any further questions and research about the hows and whys should be guided by the neurodivergent trans community.

32 Treating someone as if they are a child.

33 An intense focus for an extended period of time.

34 Changing behavior in order to reduce stigma. This can be things like imitating facial expression, holding eye contact, or limiting the amount that you discuss a certain interest.

35 Also sometimes called autistigender.

36 Not autistic.

37 Difficulty with executive functioning tasks such as time management, the ability to switch between tasks, the ability to multitask, the ability to keep track of details, and others.

38 When in doubt, googling "How to find a trans-affirming therapist in [location]" or reaching out to a local LGBTQ organization for a recommendation will probably yield enough results to get you started.

39 This can be an issue when people suggest asking your therapist their style of therapy or theoretical orientation, and, because there are so many theoretical orientations, you might get an answer you've never heard of before. Feel free to ask the question, of course, but perhaps only if you feel comfortable saying, "I've never heard of that. Can you explain what Gestalt therapy means and what it looks like in a session?" Otherwise, you are just left with some jargon that doesn't have a whole lot of significance to you.

40 The amplified experience of the intersection of transphobia and misogyny.

41 This will be discussed in greater detail in the section on intimate partner violence in Chapter 20.

42 Alternately called feminism-appropriating reactionary transphobes (FARTS).

43 A term coined by second-wave feminists to exclude trans women from attendance and membership. Seen first in 1977 by Michigan Womyn's Music Festival (Michfest) and in 1978 by the Lesbian Organization of Toronto.

44 The intersection of misogyny and racism against Black women. The term transmisogynoir is sometimes used to describe the intersection of oppression against Black trans women.

45 Transphobia and interphobia/intersexphobia can overlap and function similarly at times when people are simply attempting to negate someone's gender. Of course, trans and intersex individuals experience separate kinds of oppression, but in instances like these, the route of bigotry seems less important than the effect of negation or even dehumanization.

46 Embracing it and taking action can be entirely separate steps. You have no obligation to start making external changes on any timeline.

47 Cromwell, J. (1999) *Transmen and FTMs: Identities, Bodies, Genders, and Sexualities*. University of Illinois Press, pages 89–90.

48 Karen Horney, a female psychoanalyst, said as much. She believed that penis envy made more sense as a metaphor for women's desire for the social prestige that men have. Freud responded, "We shall not be very greatly surprised if a woman analyst who has not been sufficiently convinced of the intensity of her own wish for a penis also fails to attach proper importance to that factor in her patients," which proves that indeed Freud was a dick. Freud, S. (1940) "An outline of psycho-analysis." *The International Journal of Psychoanalysis*, 21, 27–84.

49 National Center for Transgender Equality, *2015 U.S. Transgender Survey*.

50 Unless, of course, this is an agreed upon kink dynamic with clear communication and boundaries, in which case you do you, and you're only an asshole in the context of the scene.

51 Lawrence, A.A. (2011) "Autogynephilia: an underappreciated paraphilia." *Advances in Psychosomatic Medicine*, 31, 135–148.

52 Some phrases the women were asked to respond to were: "I have dressed in lingerie, sexy attire, or prepared myself (shaving my legs, applying make-up, etc.) before masturbating"; "I have been erotically aroused by imagining myself with a 'sexier' body"; and "I have been erotically aroused by contemplating myself fully clothed in sexy attire." Moser, C. (2009) "Autogynephilia in women." *Journal of Homosexuality*, 56, 5, 539–547.

Index